ILLUSTRATED ENCYCLOPEDIA

THE COMPLETE GUIDE TO
SPIRITS &
LIQUEURS

ILLUSTRATED ENCYCLOPEDIA

THE COMPLETE GUIDE TO
SPIRITS &
LIQUEURS

STUART WALTON

HERMES
HOUSE

This edition first published by Hermes House
an imprint of
Anness Publishing Limited
Hermes House, 88-89 Blackfriars Road
London SE1 8HA

© 1998, 2000 Anness Publishing Limited

A CIP catalogue record for this book is available from the British Library

Publisher: Joanna Lorenz
Senior Editor: Linda Fraser
Copy Editor: Jane Hughes
Indexer: Hilary Bird
Designer: Sara Kidd
Photography: Janine Hosegood and David Jordan
Illustrator: Madeleine David

Previously published as *The New Guide to Spirits and Liqueurs*, and
as part of a larger compendium, *Spirits & Liqueurs Cookbook*.

Printed and bound in Hong Kong
1 3 5 7 9 10 8 6 4 2

CONTENTS

Liqueurs 58

Fortified Wines 106

Non-Alcoholic Mixers 124

Index 126

INTRODUCTION

AT WHAT POINT IN HISTORY alcoholic drinks were first used in cooking, quite apart from fulfilling their time-honoured role as intoxicants, is a question that may never be answered. It seems a fair guess, however, to suggest that it was related to the discovery of fermentation.

The ancient Egyptians used fermented grains for making prototype forms of beer. These grains also enabled them to refine the techniques for producing raised breads. It was found that adding beer sediment – which was still full of live yeasts – was the quickest and easiest method of encouraging the start of fermentation in a new batch of dough. It was still going strong in the English Middle Ages when dough fermentation was initiated by the addition of froth from the head of the finished beer. Without being fanciful, it could plausibly be argued that this use of beer in bread-making represented the first appearance of alcohol in the culinary arts.

Wine, too, played its part in the foods of classical Greece and later Rome, not initially for adding flavour but for its acidity. The action of acids in softening the fibres of tough-textured meats led to the invention of marinating, which is still an indispensable procedure in kitchens the world over for tenderizing the meat of older animals. As well as making tough meat more supple, marinating would have removed excess salt from meats that had been encrusted with it, or soaked in brine, for preservation. Wine vinegar, its alcohol lost to acetic acid, may have been the first recourse, but wine itself appears in sauce recipes in the

historically important late Roman cookery book of Apicius (3rd century AD). The wine itself was commonly infused with spices to mask the rank flavours of oxidation or acetification.

Today, adding wine to a sauce or using beer in casseroles are commonplaces of the domestic kitchen. The drinks featured in this book, however, spirits, liqueurs and fortified wines, are quite different types of drink. What they have in common is that they all depend to some degree on distillation. Even the fortified wines – sherry, port, Madeira and the others – are made stronger, and in some cases naturally sweeter, than ordinary table wine by the addition of a distillate.

Distillation (from the Latin *destillare*, to drip) is the extraction of higher alcohols from fermented drinks by using the action of heat to vapourize them. Compared to fermentation itself, distillation is a

remarkably simple process, largely because it is much more readily subject to external control. Whereas freshly pressed grape juice needs the right ambient temperature to begin the process of turning into good wine, a spirit can be produced from wine simply by applying heat to it. Alcohol has a lower boiling point than water (about 78°C compared to 100°C), so it vapourizes into steam some time before the water content in the wine starts to boil. When the alcohol-laden steam hits a cool surface, it forms a dripping condensation, and reverts to a liquid of which the alcohol constitutes a much higher proportion than it did in the wine. Boil that liquid up again, and the same procedure will yield an even higher alcohol, and so on.

Much academic debate has been generated in the last 30 years or so as to when and where distillation was first discovered. The Greek

Right: Turning the drying germinated barley in the peat kiln at Glendronach Distillery near Huntly, Banffshire, Scotland.

Right: This burbling stream provides one
of the essential ingredients for whisky
distillation – clear spring water.

philosopher Aristotle, who lived in the 4th century BC, writes of distillation as a way of purifying seawater to make it drinkable. He comments in passing that the same treatment can be given to wine, which is reduced thereby to a sort of "water". He was tantalizingly close to the break-through, but the experiment did no more than prove for him that wine is just a form of modified water, and that a liquid can only derive flavour from whatever happens to be mixed with the water that forms its base.

The documented beginnings of systematic and scientifically founded distillation, at least in Europe, come from the celebrated medical school at Salerno around 1100 AD. Wine itself was held to have a range of medicinal properties (a view that has once again found favour in the 1990s), and the extraction of what was held to be the soul or spirit of the wine, through distillation, is what led to the naming of distillates as "spirits". Alcohol was believed to be the active ingredient in the healing powers of wine. Up to that time, the word "alcohol" was applied as a generic term to any product that had been arrived at by a process of vapourizing and condensation. Its origin from the Arabic word al-kuhl refers to the Arab practice of producing a black powder by condensing a vapour of the metal antimony. The powder was then used as eye makeup, which is why eye-liner is still occasionally known as kohl. It was not until the 16th century that "alcohol" was used specifically in reference to distilled spirits.

Not only medicine but the ancient practice of alchemy were involved in the European origins of distillation. Alchemy was a respected branch of the physical sciences, and was chiefly concerned with finding a means of transforming ordinary metals into gold. It was wholeheartedly believed

that if such a process could be discovered, it might well be possible to apply it to the human body and extract the essential life force from its mortal shell, thus guaranteeing eternal youth. With the realization that alcohol could be repeatedly distilled to a greater and greater purity, it was thought that spirits could be the Holy Grail.

Although it can't have taken long for the Salerno doctors to ascertain that whatever other remarkable properties distilled spirit had, the power to confer everlasting life wasn't one of them, the medical uses of spirits were to endure for hundreds of years. It was Arnaldo de Villanova, a Catalan physician of the 13th century, who first coined the Latin term aqua vitae, "water of life", for distilled spirits, indicating that they were still held to be associated with the promotion of

vitality and health. (That term lives on in the Scandinavian aquavit, the French eau de vie and other spirituous names.)

Undoubtedly, the earliest distillates were of wine, since it had a more salubrious and exalted image than did beer, but grain distillation to produce the first whiskies and neutral spirits followed later in the Middle Ages. Many of these prototypes contained herb and spice extracts, or were flavoured with fruit, in order to enhance the medicinal properties of the preparation. The additives also conveniently masked what must have been the fairly raw taste and off-putting aroma of the unadulterated liquor. Anybody who has smelt and tasted clear spirit dribbling off the still in a brandy distillery (or, for that matter, has had a brush with illicit Irish poteen or American moonshine) will know how far such untreated spirit is from the welcoming smoothness of five-star cognac or single malt Scotch. The infused distillates were the antecedents of many of the traditional aromatic liqueurs and flavoured vodkas of today.

That, for centuries, was the official account of the birth of distilled spirits. In 1961, however, an Indian food historian, O. Prakash, argued that there was evidence that distillation of rice and barley beer was practised in India around 800 BC. Others have argued that, if so, it probably arrived there from China even earlier. Thus, current

Right: An original whisky pot still has become a museum piece at the Jameson Heritage Centre, Midleton, County Cork.

theory cautiously credits the Chinese as the discoverers of the art.

It seems unusual that distilled alcohol was not remarked on or even apparently encountered by soldiers engaged in the European invasion of

India, led by Alexander the Great in 327 BC. His campaign is reliably credited with having brought back rice itself to Europe, but any rice spirit appears to have been overlooked. Perhaps, if it was drunk at all by the invaders, it was in a diluted form, and was not therefore perceived to be any higher in alcohol than the grape wine with which they were familiar. Then again, it may just have been rejected as smelling or looking unclean. Whatever the explanation, if the Chinese or Indians did practise distillation as long ago as is claimed, the expertise they had stumbled on centuries before the Europeans remained specific to that part of the world.

The original and still widespread distillation vessel, used in the Cognac region of France, as well as by the whisky distillers of Scotland, is the pot still. It consists of the only three elements absolutely essential to the process: a pot in which the fermented product (malted grains, wine, cider, etc.) is heated; the alembic, or tube, through which the alcohol vapour driven off is sucked up; and the condenser where the steam is cooled and reliquified.

To obtain a better quality product, spirits are generally distilled at least twice for greater refinement, so the still has to be started up again. Moreover, not all of the condensed vapour is suitable for use in fine liquor. The first and last of it to pass through (known as the "heads" and "tails") are generally discarded for the relatively high level of impurities they contain. The invention of the continuous still in the early 19th century, in which the process carries on to a second distillation uninterrupted, made spirit production more economical and easier to control. This is the method used in France's other classic brandy, armagnac, and it is now the preferred apparatus for most spirits production worldwide.

Above: The final character, precise colour, and the richness and roundness of flavour of both cognac and whisky are derived from the final maturation period in wood.

Left: Copper pot stills – the original distilla-tion vessel – are widely used in the Cognac region of France as well as by the whisky distillers of Scotland.

Probably the first spirit to be taken seriously as an object of connoisseurship, as distinct from being purely medicinal or just a method of using up surplus grape or grain production, was the brandy of the Cognac region of western France. It was noticed that the superior, mellower spirit produced by the light wines of Cognac responded particularly well to ageing in oak casks. The casks were traditionally fashioned out of wood from the Limousin forests of the region. Cask-aged spirits derive every bit of their final character, from the precise shade of tawny in the colour to their richness and roundness of flavour, from the maturation period they undergo in wood. They will not continue to develop in the bottle. The complex classification system in operation today for cognac is based on the length of time the spirit has been aged. It is testimony to a reputation for painstaking quality that dates back to around the end of the 1600s.

Scottish and Irish whiskies rose to similar prominence soon after. Their differing production processes resulted in distinct regional styles, depending on the quantities of peat used in the kilns where the malted grain is dried, on the quality of the spring water used in the mash and, some have claimed, on the shape of the still.

Varieties of whisky are made across the world these days, from North America to Japan, but all attempts to replicate the precise taste of great Scotch – for all that the ingredients and procedures may be identical – have inexplicably foundered.

Where a distilled drink stops being a spirit and turns into a liqueur is something of an elusive question. The one constant is that, to be a liqueur, a drink should have some obvious aromatizing element (perhaps even a hundred or more in the case of certain celebrated products). This doesn't mean that all flavoured distillates are liqueurs – flavoured vodkas are still vodka – but there are no neutral liqueurs. Some of these products have histories at least as venerable as those of cognac and Scotch. The most notable are those produced by the old French monastic orders. Bénédictine, the cognac-based, herb-scented potion that originated at the monastery in

Above: The all-important water that flows through an old-fashioned water wheel at a traditional distillery in Northern Ireland.

Fécamp, in Normandy, can convincingly lay claim to a lineage that rolls back to the beginning of the 16th century.

The first and greatest cocktail era, that arrived with the advent of the Jazz Age in the 1920s, rescued a lot of the traditional liqueurs from the niches of obscurity into which popular taste had relegated them. The Bénédictine monks may have been a little shocked to hear that their revered creation was being mixed with English gin, American applejack, apricot brandy and maple syrup, shaken to within an inch of its life and then rechristened the Mule's Hind Leg, but at least it was drunk – as were the giggling flappers after knocking back three or four of them.

In this book, we shall look at the histories and compositions of all of the most important spirits, liqueurs and fortified wines.

SPIRITS

THE EARLIEST SPIRITS were almost certainly fairly straightforward, rough-and-ready distillations of ordinary wine. For centuries, a form of distillation had been practised using herbs and flowers infused in water, then cooked and condensed. The resulting essence was used medicinally, in cooking or just as a perfume. As we saw in the Introduction, the discovery in Europe of the art of distilling alcohol arose as a result of alchemical experiments designed to find the "elixir of life". The powerful brew that was arrived at by distilling was thought to contain the "soul" or "spirit" of the wine.

When it was realized that anything that had been fermented to produce alcohol could in turn be distilled into spirit, the process came to be applied to materials that were fermented *specifically* for distillation, rather than being consumable products in themselves. So, mashed malted grains were responsible, in regions that lacked the climate for wine-making, for the first drinks definable as whiskies.

As wine itself was held in high esteem, and was imported in great quantity by the cooler countries of northern Europe, such as England and Holland, the spirit produced from wine was the first to receive true acclaim. Traders on ships putting in at La Rochelle and other ports in the Charente region of western France had no particular taste for the acidic, flavourless wines of the area, but the strong spirit the wines could be turned into was considered a lot better than other such distillates found elsewhere. Thus did cognac first come to prominence.

A memory of the alchemical quest to find the magic elixir was preserved in the Latin name first given to the product of distillation: *aqua vitae*, water of life. That phrase has remained inseparable from spirits terminology: the French call their spirit *eau-de-vie,* the Scandinavians *aquavit*, and the Celts *uisge beatha*, which was eventually corrupted by non-Gaelic speakers into whisky. In Russian, it became, more humbly, "little water" or vodka. The alternative medieval Latin name was *aqua ardens*, "burning water", for reasons that are not hard to fathom. The association with fieriness, both in the method used to extract the alcohol and in the sensation that drinking it produced, lived on in the naming of distilled wine *Gebranntwein* ("burnt

Above left: Scotland's smallest distillery in Pitlochry, Scotland was built in 1837.

Below left: Traditionally whisky was aged in used oak sherry casks.

Below: The dark berries of the juniper tree contribute the characteristic perfume of gin.

wine") in German, *brandewijn* in Dutch and eventually brandy in English.

Despite being highly prized, these early spirits would not have tasted particularly pleasant to us. They would only have been distilled once and would therefore have contained high concentrations of fusel oil, a group of compounds known in scientific parlance as the "higher alcohols", the "higher" referring to their greater acidity. It was only in 1800 that a physicist named Adam discovered the benefits of redistillation or rectification. This dispensed with a large proportion, though not all, of the raw-tasting higher alcohols and resulted in a purer spirit. It also stripped away a lot of the positive by-products of distillation that gave the drink its character, and so for a while the infusions of herbs, spices and fruit extracts that had originally been used to disguise the roughness of the

alcohol came back into favour in order to give it flavour.

Eventually, the correct balance was struck. The products that needed some distillation character – brandies and whiskies – retained it (undergoing a double distillation) and had it enhanced by ageing in wooden casks, while those that were intended to be as neutral as possible, such as vodka and gin, were subject to repeated redistillation. (In the case of gin and similar products, a neutral spirit base is created by prolonged rectification, so that the aromatic ingredients that are added can stand out the more boldly.) Most commercial spirits produced today have been thoroughly rectified, which is not necessarily a blessing: one thinks of the relentless blandness of some brands of white rum. The trend owes much to the fact that most of the white spirits are drunk with mixers these days.

Above: This modern distillery produces the neutral spirit base for both gin and vodka.

When tasting a fine spirit – aged cognac, single malt whisky, sour-mash bourbon or old demerara rum, for example – the procedure that is used for tasting wine clearly won't do. Try rolling a liquid with 40% alcohol around your mouth and you'll soon wish you hadn't. Some tasters judge them on the nose alone; others add a similar quantity of water, which many feel emphasizes their aromatic subtleties. I prefer to be brave and taste them undiluted. If you follow this route, the trick is to take in only a very little liquid, keep it at the front of the mouth just behind the lips by lowering the head after sipping, draw some air over it quickly and spit it out before it starts burning. The whole exercise is much brisker than tasting a mouthful of wine.

AQUAVIT

AMONG THE VARIOUS spirits whose collective names are derived from the phrase "water of life", Scandinavian aquavit or akvavit has a particularly ancient history. It is known to have been distilled in northern Europe since medieval times, and its use as a drink – as distinct from its purely medical application – dates back at least to the 15th century.

Production of aquavit is very similar to that of flavoured vodkas. Its base is a neutral grain and/or potato spirit, which is rectified to a high degree of purity and then aromatized, usually with fragrant spices. The Scandinavian countries and Germany are the production centres of true aquavit. Its alternative name, schnapps, derives from an old Nordic verb *snappen*, meaning to snatch or seize. It denotes the way in which it is traditionally drunk, snatched down the throat in a single gulp.

HOW IT IS MADE
Potatoes are boiled in a contraption rather like a huge pressure-cooker, and the resulting starchy mass is then mixed with malted grains. After fermentation with yeasts, it is double-distilled to obtain a neutral spirit. Dilution brings it down to a drinkable strength, and contact with charcoal – as well as the accepted flavouring elements – gives it its final character.

AALBORG
A premium high-strength aquavit from Denmark

TASTES GOOD WITH
Despite its cinematic association with reckless drinking sessions, aquavit has a genuine gastronomic history. It formed an integral part of the original Swedish *smörgåsbord*, which was a more modest feast than the lavish spreads of today. It consisted of just bread, fish (generally herring) and perhaps cheese, washed down with aquavit. The dry savouriness of the spirit complemented the appetizing role of the salty food. Divorced from its edible accompaniments, aquavit lives on today as an aperitif, knocked back in one and followed by a chaser of local beer.

PEACH COUNTY SCHNAPPS
A mild fruit-flavoured commercial schnapps

ARAK

ALTHOUGH THE DISCOVERY of distillation is still hotly disputed, it is just possible that some form of arak, or raki, was the very first spirit. There are claims that it was made in India around 800 BC, and certainly the production of a fiery, clear spirit on the sub-continent, and down in the South Pacific too, goes back many centuries.

Arak is not really one drink, but a generic name for a group of clear distillates, for which the base material and method of production vary according to the region of origin. In Java, Sumatra and Borneo, the fermented juice of sugar-cane provides the base, but there are also rice versions. The sap of palm trees, which ferments very readily in sultry temperatures, is popular as a source of arak in India.

The drink came to the Middle East and the Mediterranean with the

RAKI
Simple Turkish raki
that has not been
cask-aged

OTHER NAMES
Arrack, arraki, racki, raki, rakija

HOW TO SERVE
Like aquavit, arak or raki should be drunk in fairly abstemious measures. Owing to its rough potency, arak is not generally served chilled, and it is safer to sip it appreciatively rather than down it in one.

FLAVOURINGS
Figs, dates, grapes, raisins and plums

early Arab spice trade; its common name is derived from the Arabic word for juice or sap, *araq*. Other easily fermentable products such as dates and figs gradually infiltrated the making of arak, and are still used in parts of North Africa and the Middle East. Finally, grape wine came to play its part in the old wine-making cultures of Greece and Cyprus, including that made from raisins.

In the West today, arak is most commonly encountered in the form of raki, the aniseed-tinged spirit of Greece and Turkey. Some coloured raki is very fine, and is based on old cask-aged brandies, but most is a colourless and pretty raw-tasting spirit that can be anything up to 50% alcohol by volume (ABV). Raki is made throughout the Balkan countries of southeast Europe, sometimes from figs or plums rather than grapes.

TASTES GOOD WITH
Around the Mediterranean region, raki is nearly always drunk as an aperitif, but if you are lucky enough to find a particularly mellow example, it may be better drunk at the latter end of the meal, after coffee.

MIXING
If drunk as an appetizer, the more basic grade of raki may well be taken with ice in Greece and Cyprus.

BITTERS

FLAVOURINGS

Numerous herbs and roots impart greater or lesser degrees of bitterness to all of these drinks.

Gentian is quite common. It is a flowering alpine plant, the root of which is rendered down to a bright yellow essence that has been used as a tonic and anti-fever remedy in folk medicine for centuries.

Quinine was the New World alternative to gentian. It is an extract of the bark of the cinchona tree, a native of South America.

Seville oranges The dried peel of this bitter variety is essential in Campari.

THE TERM "BITTERS" refers to any one of a number of spirits flavoured with bitter herbs or roots, which are generally held to have medicinal properties. They range from products such as Campari, which can be drunk in whole measures like any other spirit, to those that are so bitter that they are only added in drops to season another drink.

Bitterness is the last of the four main taste sensations (the others being sweetness, saltiness and sourness) that developing tastebuds learn to appreciate. A fondness for bitter flavours is often thought to be a sign of the palate having reached its true maturity.

The link between bitterness and health is evident in the fact that tonic water was originally conceived as an all-purpose pick-me-up containing the stimulant quinine, rather than as a mixer for gin, although these days its flavour tends to be drowned with artificial sweetening. The other unquestionably effective medicinal role of bitters is as an aid to digestion.

The origins of bitters lie in the flavouring elements that were commonly added to the very earliest spirits. These elixirs were taken as restoratives and remedies for any number of conditions, ranging from poor digestion to painful joints. The apothecaries who concocted them drew on the collected wisdom of herbal medicine, and added extracts of bark, roots, fruit peels, herbs and spices to enhance the healing powers of the drink.

Bitters are made all over the world. Perhaps the most famous of all is Angostura. An infusion of gentian root with herbs on a strong rum base, Angostura was invented in the 19th century by a German medic who was personal doctor to the South American revolutionary hero Simón Bolívar. He named it after a town in Venezuela, although today it is made exclusively in Trinidad, albeit still by the company founded by its inventor. Angostura is one of the few such medicinal drinks that can lay claim to actually having been formulated by a doctor.

In Europe the two major centres of production

UNDERBERG
An intensely pungent digestive bitter from Germany

CAMPARI
Italy's most famous bitter aperitif also comes in a ready-mixed bottle with a crown cap

MIXING

Negroni: Thoroughly mix equal measures of gin, Campari and sweet red vermouth with ice in a tumbler and add a squirt of soda.
Americano: As for Negroni, but leave out the gin and add a few drops of Angostura.
Pink gin (below): Sprinkle about half-a-dozen drops of Angostura into a goblet-shaped glass, roll it around to coat the inner surfaces, then dash it out. Add ice-cold gin, which will then take on the faintest pink tint.

of bitters are Italy and France. Italy has Campari – a bright red aperitif of uncompromising bitterness, which is made in Milan – and also Fernet-Branca. Like Germany's Underberg, it is sold in little bottles and is often recommended as a hangover cure. France's famous bitters include Amer Picon (which was invented as an anti-malarial remedy by an army officer serving in Algeria), Toni-Kola and Secrestat.

English fruit bitters, such as orange and peach, were widely used in the cocktail era of the 1920s. Hungary's runner is Unicum, which balances its bitterness with a slight sweetness, while the Latvians add their own treacle-dark dry tonic, Melnais Balzams (Black Balsam), to their coffee.

FERNET-BRANCA
The Italian bitter much prized as a hangover cure

UNICUM
A deeply coloured bitter speciality of Hungary

ANGOSTURA
The most widely used bitter in the cocktail repertoire

HOW TO SERVE

Campari is classically served with soda water and a twist of lemon peel, but don't drown it. Amer Picon may be served the same way, or perhaps as a bittering element with gin for those whose need to be picked up requires more than a straight dry Martini. Underberg and Fernet-Branca can be quaffed straight as stomach-settlers or just to aid digestion, while Angostura is essential in a pink gin – the drink of officers and gentlemen.

BRANDY

STRICTLY SPEAKING, the term brandy applies to any grape-based spirit distilled from wine. There are "brandies" made from other fruits – such as Normandy's calvados, made from apples – but we shall deal with these under their own headings. The English name is a corruption of the Dutch *brandewijn*, in turn derived from the German *Gebranntwein*, meaning burnt wine, which is an apt term for the product of distillation.

The most famous of all true brandies is cognac, named after a town in the Charente region of western France. It was to here that traders from northern Europe, particularly the Netherlands, came in the 17th century, putting in at the port of La Rochelle to take delivery of consignments of salt. They inevitably took some of the region's thin, acidic wine with them as well. Because of tax regulations, and to save space in the ships' holds – always a major consideration – the wines were boiled to reduce their volume by evaporation. On arrival at their destination, they would be reconstituted with water. However, it came to be noticed that the Charente wines positively benefited from the reduction process. It was but a short step from there to actual distillation.

HOW TO SERVE

Fine cognac should be drunk just as it comes, without mixers and certainly without ice. It is traditionally served in balloon glasses that allow room for swirling. Tradition is not often a reliable guide, and the aromas are much better appreciated in something resembling a large liqueur glass, which mutes the prickle of the spirit. The bouquet is also encouraged by a gentle warming of the glass in the hand (for which the balloon was indisputably better designed), but recourse to those lovely, old, silver brandy-warmers, which allowed you to barbecue the tilted glass over a little petrol flame, is not recommended.

Such was the fame and the premium paid for the distilled wines of the Charente that they came to have many imitators. None, however, could match the precise local conditions in which cognac is made. Its chalky soils, the maritime climate and the ageing in barrels fashioned from Limousin oak were the indispensable features that gave cognac the pre-eminent reputation that it enjoys to this day.

France's other brandy of note, armagnac, is made in the southwest of the country. Armagnac is based on a wider range of grape varieties and made using a slightly different method to cognac. Although not as widely known as cognac, it has its own special cachet in the spirits market and is preferred by many as the better digestif.

MARTELL
The oldest house in Cognac is still a brand leader

There are grape brandies produced all over Europe and the Americas, as we shall see in the succeeding pages. The best are generally made by the pot-still method of distillation. Some inferior spirit, artificially coloured and flavoured, used also to be known as brandy, but has been banned from using the term within the European Union following the introduction of a new law in 1989.

COGNAC

The Cognac region covers two *départements* on the western side of France near the Bay of Biscay: inland Charente, and Charente-Maritime on the coast. Cognac is a small town close to the border between the two. The vineyards are sub-divided into six growing areas, the most notable of which are Grande Champagne and Petite Champagne, just south of Cognac itself.

As we have seen, the fame of cognac had been well and truly established in the Dutch and British markets by the end of

HENNESSY X.O
Premium cognac in a singularly shaped decorative bottle

the 17th century. The industry's first great entrepreneur was Jean Martell, a Jersey-born opportunist who, in 1715, turned away from a life of crime (smuggling) in order to found the house that still bears his name. Cognac's other leading brands are Hennessy, Courvoisier and Rémy Martin. Smaller but no less distinguished companies include Hine and Otard.

The relative qualities of different cognacs depend almost entirely on the length of time they have been aged and the cognacs are classified accordingly. No brandy that has earned the right to the Cognac *appellation contrôlée* (AC) status may be blended from spirits that are less than two years old. At the bottom rung of the quality classification for the British and Irish markets is VS (historically known as three-star, and still designated by a row of three stars on the label). VS may contain brandies as young as three years old, but the basic products of most of the leading companies will contain some significantly older reserves.

The next stage up is VSOP, Very Special (or Superior) Old Pale, an old British term that arose in London in the 19th century to denote a particularly fine – but paradoxically light-coloured – batch of cognac. (Although cognac derives most of its colour from wood-ageing, caramel can also be added to influence the colour, provided it does not affect the taste. Any slight sweetness in the spirit derives from correction with sugar solution just before bottling.) VSOP is the five-star stuff because the youngest spirit it contains must have spent at least five years in wood.

Those blended from minimum six-year-old cognacs may be entitled XO, or given any one of a number of names the houses invent for themselves, such as Reserve, Extra, Cordon Bleu, Paradis or classically Napoléon – so named because the bottles supposedly contain brandies aged since the time of the *Empéreur*.

The prices that the oldest cognacs command are breathtaking, yet the enjoyment can never be proportionately greater than that to be had from good VSOP. In many cases, you may be paying for something that looks like a giant perfume

COURVOISIER
Along with Martell, this is one of the most widely drunk cognacs in the world.

REMY MARTIN
The basic Rémy is a VSOP grade of cognac.

bottle fashioned in cut crystal and presented in a silk-lined box. If you really want to try one of these luxury products, it makes sense to wait until your next trip through duty-free.

It is often thought that the optimum age for the best cognacs is about 40 years old, but it must always be borne in mind with any spirit that it can only age in cask. Once it is bottled, no further development takes place.

ARMAGNAC

Armagnac, which was thought of until about the middle of the 19th century merely as France's "other brandy", is made in the Pays de Gascogne in the far southwest of the country. There are three sub-regions – Bas-Armagnac, Ténarèze and Haut-Armagnac – of which the first is usually

NAMING

"Brandy" is just a generic term for any distilled grape spirit. They get very upset in Cognac and Armagnac these days, and perhaps understandably, if you refer to their products unceremoniously as brandy. It is happily used by quality producers in Spain, California and elsewhere. Note that none of these products contains any added flavouring element. If they do, they cease to be "brandy", at least in terms of the European Union definition of 1989.

ARMAGNAC
"Hors d'Age" on an armagnac label denotes very long cask-ageing

considered the best. Despite its lesser renown, armagnac has a legitimate claim to be considered the more venerable product, distillation in the region having been reliably dated back to the 1400s. Its chief distinguishing characteristics compared to cognac are these: while cognac is made largely from the Ugni Blanc grape, armagnac's base wine is made from a blend of several varieties; a local black oak (as distinct from Limousin) is used for the maturation; and the continuous still (invented by Edouard Adam) is widely used to distil the spirit.

So inextricably bound up with armagnac production was Adam's patent still that, for a long period this century, it was the only authorized apparatus for producing armagnac. Continuous distillation yields a spirit rich in the aroma-containing impurities that give any brandy its character, which is why armagnac is noticeably more fragrant than cognac. Many tasters describe it as having a "biscuity" aroma, while others – by no means fancifully – detect a floral topnote like violets. The flavour tends to be drier because it isn't adjusted with sugar, and the absence of caramel as a colouring matter makes it generally paler than a cognac of the same age.

The labelling system is comparable to that of cognac. The exception is that the youngest armagnacs may be released in the British market after two years in cask rather than three. The designations VS, VSOP and XO are defined in exactly the same way. Vintage-dated armagnac – the unblended produce of a single year's harvest – has always been a peculiarity of the region (although vintage labelling has just been relegalized in Cognac). If the label on, say, a 1959 armagnac looks suspiciously new, remember that it is because it has probably only recently been bottled. The ageing can only take place in wood, not glass.

Part of the charm of the Armagnac region is that many of the producers are still rural artisans, rather than globally important companies catering to the luxury market, as in Cognac. Their brandies are often distilled in shared portable stills that are driven around the countryside at production time. As a result, prices for even the top armagnacs are considerably gentler.

OTHER EUROPEAN BRANDIES

Spain The most significant producer of grape brandy, in terms of both quantity and quality, outside France is Spain. The premium products are accorded the same attention to detail at every stage of their manufacture as the finest in Cognac and Armagnac and, as a result, are fully capable of withstanding comparison with their French counterparts.

Spanish brandy production is concentrated in the sherry region of Jerez, in the south of the country. Indeed, most of it is distilled by the sherry houses, such as Gonzalez Byass, Domecq and Osborne. The grapes from which the base wine is made generally come from La Mancha, the huge central plain that represents the grape basket of Spanish viticulture, but the wines are distilled and aged in sherry country. This entitles them to the designation of Brandy de Jerez – a dependable indicator of quality.

Maturation is by a process known as fractional blending, or the *solera* system, which is also used for the finest sherries. A *solera* consists of a stack of barrels piled up in rows. The new spirit enters the top row and, at intervals of several months, a quantity of it is drawn off and added to the next row down, where it displaces a similar quantity into the row below, and so on. The bottom row contains the oldest brandies which are drawn off in fractions for bottling.

LEPANTO
Spain's leading brandy, made by Gonzalez Byass of sherry fame

The brandy gains greater age characteristics by this process than it would if it were left to mature undisturbed in the same barrel, as in France, for a similar period.

Top brands include Lepanto, made by Gonzalez Byass, Sanchez Romate's Cardinal Mendoza and Osborne's Conde d'Osborne, which comes in an idiosyncratically shaped bottle designed by the mad genius of 20th-century Spanish art, Salvador Dali. The brand leader, though, is Fundador, a Domecq product, and one that deserves a much better reputation. In Catalonia, the pace-setting Torres winery makes its own very drinkable brandy.

Germany The best German offering seen on export markets is Uralt, an aged product made by a distiller in the Rheingau called Asbach. It receives a maturation period of around 18 months. Like the country's less good sparkling wines, most German brandy is made from imported French or Italian base wine, and so it has no particular indigenous character.

Others Italy's brandies are fairly basic commercial spirits, most coming from the volume producer Stock. Portugal makes a handful of good brandies, but its industry is heavily geared to supplying grape spirit for the port shippers. In southeast Europe, Cyprus makes brandies of about the same level of sophistication as the fortified wines it once called "sherry", while Bulgaria still produces a decent aged brandy from base wine principally derived from the Ugni Blanc grape of Cognac.

METAXA

Among the brandies produced on the mainland of Greece (and to some extent on the island of Samos), the abidingly popular Metaxa deserves a special mention. Despite the brouhaha with which it is treated in Greece itself, and a distinctly specious system of age-labelling, it is a fairly basic industrial product.

Greek brandy isn't ever going to fare well against aged cognac for the simple reason that the grape varieties that go into it are not generally of sufficiently high acidity to produce a suitable base wine. The mainstays are Savatiano (widely used in retsina) and the Muscat grape that produces the golden dessert wines of Samos and other islands, and the distillers are not above using base wines that contain some red grapes.

There are three grades of Metaxa, ascending in quality from three stars to five and seven. The last is sometimes said to have been cask-aged for around half a century, a claim we can confidently take with a cask of salt. It is relatively pale in colour (which fact alone makes the age claim suspicious) and much sweeter on the palate than cognac, with a highly moreish toffee or caramel quality.

AMERICAN BRANDIES

USA Brandy has been made in the United States since the days of the pioneers, most of it in what is now the premier wine-growing state of California. At one time, brandy production was simply a convenient means of using up sub-standard grapes that were considered unfit for quality wine production, as it still is in many of Europe's viticultural regions. In the last 30 years or so, however, a turn towards producing finer aged spirits has been made, and a number of these American products are capable of giving some of the famous VSOP cognacs a run for their money.

Not all are made in the image of cognac; some are discernibly more orientated towards the Spanish style. The brandies are habitually matured in barrels of home-grown American oak,

METAXA
The holiday maker's favourite brandy

CARNEROS ALAMBIC
Brandy from the Napa Valley, California

MIXING

Brandy Blazer: Put two measures of cognac in a saucepan with one sugar cube and the thinly pared rind from half an orange and one lemon. Heat gently, then remove from the heat and light the surface of the liquid. The alcohol will burn with a low, blue flame for about one minute. Blow out the flame. Add half a measure of Kahlúa and strain into a heat-resistant liqueur glass. Decorate with a cocktail stick threaded with a twist of orange rind.

which gives a more pronounced aroma to the spirit, accentuated by the heavily charred inner surfaces of the barrels. These conditions result in brandies of great richness and complexity. Names to look out for include Germain-Robin and RMS (the latter brand owned by Cognac star Rémy Martin). Some of the top California wineries have also turned out some impressive efforts, while bulk producer Gallo in Modesto make a passable version intended for mixing.

Latin America There is a long tradition of drinking fiery spirits all over Central and South America, in which grape brandy plays its part – particularly in the areas where the early Spanish colonists first planted vines. Mexico is the most important producer. Its flagship is a big-selling global brand called Presidente, made in the light, simple style of a rough-and-ready Spanish brandy.

The peculiarly South American offering, however, is pisco. There is still much dispute over whether it originated in Peru or Chile, the two centres of production (with a modest

contribution from Bolivia). I shall forbear to come down on either side of the fence, except to point out that the Pisco valley and the seaport of the same name are in Peru, but the Chileans simply insist that that was one of the principal export destinations for their indigenous spirit, and the name just stuck.

Despite receiving some cask-ageing, pisco is always colourless because the barrels it matures in are so ancient that they have no colour left to give to the spirit. In Chile, the longer the maturation, the lower the dilution before bottling, so the finer grades (Gran Pisco is the best) are the strongest. Owing to widespread use of members of the Muscat grape family in the base wine, nearly all types and nationalities of pisco are marked by an unabashed fruitiness on the nose and palate.

The myth that pisco is a throat-searing firewater strictly for the peasants is probably based on the exposure of delicate European sensibilities to the lower grades. Top pisco has every right to be considered a world-class spirit.

PISCO
A top-quality
pisco from Peru

MIXING

Pisco Sour: Half-fill a small tumbler with smashed ice. Put in two measures of freshly squeezed lime juice and sweeten to taste with icing sugar. Stir well to dissolve the sugar. Add a measure of pisco, and give the drink a final stir.

CALVADOS

I N AREAS WHERE wine grapes could not be grown with success, other fruits came to supplement grains in making fermented and distilled drinks. The most important fruit, after grapes, to act as a source of alcohol is the apple. Apple trees are capable of fruiting in much more wintry conditions than the vine, and since many varieties of apple are too tart or bitter to give much pleasure as eating apples, cider became the obvious alternative to beer in the cooler northern climates.

The distillation of cider is probably quite as old as the practice of distilling wine for grape brandy. In its heartland – the Normandy region of northern France – the earliest reference to an apple distillate dates from 1553, but we have no means of knowing how long, prior to the mid-1500s, it had already been going on.

If the name of the Normans' apple brandy, *calvados*, sounds more Spanish than French, that is because it derives from a story that tells of a ship, the *El Salvador*, from the mighty Spanish armada, which was dashed to smithereens off

OTHER NAMES
USA: applejack
UK: apple brandy/cider brandy

the Norman coast. The *département* came to be known as Calvados, and its traditional spirit was named after it. There is no historical corroboration of the story, and no one in Normandy seemingly expects you to believe it.

Like cognac and armagnac, calvados received its *appellation contrôlée* status quite soon after the introduction of the AC system: 1942. At the heart of the region is one particularly fine area called the Pays d'Auge, prized for its soils and the lie of its land, which has its own designation. (The rest is straight appellation Calvados.) Both the pot-still double distillation and the continuous method are used, although the calvados of the Pays d'Auge area may only use the former.

There are hundreds of different varieties of cider apple, classified into four broad taste groups: sweet, bitter-sweet, bitter and acid. The bitter-sweet ones make up the lion's share of the blend in a typical calvados. After distillation, the spirit goes into variously sized barrels of French oak for maturation. Supposedly, the younger a calvados is, the more likely it is to smell and

HOW TO SERVE
Younger calvados works surprisingly well with tonic, as long as you don't drown it. (I prefer half-and-half to one third-two thirds.) Hors d'Age, etc., must be drunk unmixed.

CALVADOS
The best calvados comes from the Pays d'Auge

APPLE BRANDY
A fine, powerful apple spirit from Somerset, England

taste of apples; the older ones take on the vanilla and spice tones of the wood.

Age indications are not dissimilar to those of cognac and armagnac. Three-star (or three-apple) calvados spends a minimum of two years in cask, Vieux or Réserve three years, and Vieille Réserve or VSOP four years. Those aged for six or more years may be labelled Hors d'Age or Age Inconnu ("age unknown"!). If a calvados is labelled with a period of ageing, such as 8-year-old, then the age specified refers to the youngest spirit in it, not the average. Should you come across any of the small amount of vintage-dated calvados, note that the date refers to the year of distillation – the year *after* harvest.

In the United States, an apple spirit has been made ever since the first British settlers found that the apple trees they planted in New England proved hardier than grain crops. Applejack, as it is most commonly known, is made in much the same way as calvados, starting with good cider and distilling it twice in a pot still. The spirit is then aged in oak for anything up to about five years. The younger stuff is pretty abrasive, but on the eastern seaboard – as in Normandy – they like it that way. Laird's is one of the bigger-selling brands.

The alternative way of making applejack, now officially frowned on, was to freeze the cider. Water freezes before alcohol, so if the first slush to form was skimmed away, what was left would be virtually pure alcohol. (A derivative of this technique is used today in the making of both ice beers and ice ciders in order to strengthen them.)

Apple brandy, or cider brandy, is now being revived in the west of England. Somerset is, after all, considered by many to be capable of producing the world's best ciders. When properly aged, it can be quite impressive, although devotees of calvados are unlikely to be fooled by it in a blind tasting.

HOW IT IS MADE

Apples are harvested from September through to December, depending on the variety. A precise blend of juices from the four types is fermented into cider at about 5–6% alcohol. This is subjected to a double distillation (or continuous distillation, except in the Pays d'Auge region of Calvados). The spirit is then aged in cask for anything up to 40 years, and bottled at 40–45% ABV.

APPLEJACK
America's answer
to calvados

EAU DE VIE

FLAVOURINGS
Numerous fruits, including strawberries, raspberries, pears, plums, bilberries, blackberries

EAU DE VIE IS the French phrase for the Latin *aqua vitae*, water of life. Strictly speaking, the term refers to all spirits distilled from fermented fruits, starting with wine-based cognac and armagnac. By the same token, calvados could therefore be considered an eau de vie of cider. Since the names of these individual spirits are legally protected by France's geographical *appellation contrôlée* regulations, they have come to be known by those names instead of being referred to as eaux de vie.

Spirits can be produced from many other fruits as well as grapes or apples, though, and these are

OTHER NAMES
The French also call colourless fruit brandies *alcools blancs*, or white spirits. Some of the fruit names in French are *framboise* (raspberry), *mûre* (blackberry), *pruneau* (plum), *poire* (pear), *fraise* (strawberry) and *myrtille* (bilberry)

much less precisely defined. The term eau de vie, therefore, tends now to be reserved for these other fruit brandies. Apart from their basic ingredients, the main attribute that distinguishes eaux de vie from cognac and armagnac is that they are colourless because they haven't been aged in wood like their more famous cousins. The theory is

HOW TO SERVE
Eaux de vie should be served extremely well chilled and neat. They blend well with neutral mixers like soda, but anything flavoured should be avoided because it will mask the attractiveness of the fruit aromas.

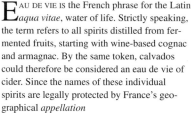

LA VIELLE PRUNE
Pascall makes this celebrated plum eau de vie

POIRE-WILLIAMS
Eau de vie flavoured with William pears

that they develop in glass, which rather flies in the face of what is scientifically known about spirits – namely, that development stops once they are in the bottle.

Of the variety of fruits used, the most often encountered – and those producing the most delicious eaux de vie – are the various soft summer berries. Alsace, a wine region of northeast France that has lurched from French to German domination and back again since the late 19th century, is a particularly rich source of these spirits. Some of them are made by winemakers, others by specialist distillers. What they have

in common is high alcohol (sometimes around 45% ABV), absence of colour and a clear, pure scent and flavour of their founding fruit. They are not sweetened, and should not be confused with the syrupy liqueurs of the same flavours, which tend to be coloured anyway.

Eau de vie of this kind is also made in Switzerland and Germany.

TASTES GOOD WITH

Served very cold in small measures, they can work well with certain desserts, particularly frangipane-based tarts topped with the same fruit as that used to make the eau de vie.

EAUX DE VIE
Three of the not-so-common types – mirabelle, fleur de bière and kirsch – are available in miniature bottles

*FRAMBOISE
SAUVAGE*
*Eau de vie
flavoured with
wild raspberries*

FRAISE
*A popular
eau de vie from
strawberries*

GIN

OF THE FIVE essential spirits (brandy, whisky, rum, vodka and gin), gin is the only one that really has a reputation to live down. Down the years it has been the calamitous curse of the urban poor, the Mother's Ruin by which young girls in trouble tried to inflict miscarriages upon themselves, the bathtub brew that rotted guts during American Prohibition, and the first resort of the miserable as the storm-clouds of depression gathered. It was all so different in the beginning.

Although the English often claim to be the true progenitors of gin (as well as, more convincingly, of port and champagne), its origins in fact go back to 16th-century Holland. Like many other distilled drinks, the first inspiration behind the creation of gin was medicinal. The blend of herbs and aromatics used in it were believed to guard against all the ills that flesh was heir to. Principal among the elements of these concoctions was juniper, the Dutch word

OTHER NAMES
Holland: genever *France*: genièvre (although almost everybody in France now calls it "gin")

for which – genever – is the linguistic root of the English word "gin".

The dark little berries of the juniper tree contribute to the characteristic strong perfume of gin. They are prized medicinally as a diuretic, to counteract water retention. Despite the predominance of juniper in the aroma and flavour of gin, however, it is not the only added ingredient. Precise recipes vary according to the individual distiller – they each have their own secret formulae – but other common components include angelica, liquorice, orris root, dried citrus peel, and caraway and coriander seeds.

HOW TO SERVE
The age-old mixer for gin is of course Schweppes tonic, the production of which is almost exclusively sustained by gin-drinkers. A gin and tonic is usually offered as a long drink with a slice of lemon and plenty of ice, but equal measures is a more sensitive way of treating the gin. Gin rubs along with any old mixer, though: orange juice, bitter lemon, ginger beer, whatever. (It isn't very nice with cola perhaps, but then few things are.)

BOMBAY SAPPHIRE
More delicately aromatic gin than the commercial norm

GORDON'S
This is the brand leader among London gins

MIXING

The number of gin-based cocktails is legion, but here are a few of the more durable ones:

Gin Fizz: Shake a good measure of gin with a teaspoon of caster sugar and the juice of half a lemon. Pour into a tall glass and top with fresh soda water. (This is not noticeably different to a **Tom Collins**, except that the latter may have a little less soda added. Then again, leave out the soda altogether, stir it in a tumbler rather than shaking it and call it a **Gin Sour**.)

Gimlet (below): Stir equal measures of Plymouth gin and Rose's lime cordial in a tumbler with a couple of ice cubes.

reform of the excise system then produced an anomaly whereby beer was suddenly subjected to a much stricter levy than before, so that gin was actually cheaper. Not surprisingly, it became the staple drink of the poorest classes, who consumed it in much the same quantities as they had beer. The gin shops were born, and public drunkenness and alcohol-related illnesses soared.

For the great mass of the London poor, getting "blotto" was the only way of escaping grim reality. So began gin's long association with gloom and despond (which still persists today in the enduring myth that gin is more of a depressant than the other spirits). The purveyors of gin sold their wares in terms that no

BELGRAVIA
LONDON
DRY GIN
One of the
lesser-known
London
brands

It may well have been British soldiers returning home from the Thirty Years' War who first brought the taste for Dutch genever across the North Sea. Then again, it may simply have been travellers to the continent starting or ending their journeys in Amsterdam. However that may be, a form of gin was being distilled in London in the 17th century, using the basic beer ingredients – hops and barley – and the essential juniper berries.

The meteoric rise in gin's popularity in Britain had two main causes. Firstly, periodic hostilities with the French led to the application of punitive tariffs to their exports and, just as port came to be the wine of patriotic choice among the elite, so gin replaced cognac. To compound that,

MIXING

Gin Rickey: Half-fill a tall glass with ice. Add two measures of gin, the juice of half a lime or a quarter of a lemon and a generous dash of grenadine. Stir vigorously, then top with fresh soda.

White Lady: Shake a measure of gin with half a measure of Cointreau and half a measure of fresh lemon juice, with ice, and strain into a cocktail glass. (Some recipes also add a teaspoon of egg white. My bible, the *Savoy Cocktail Book*, clearly indicates the White Lady to be innocent of such a substance. It simply gives the drink a frothier texture, if that's what you like.)

FLAVOURINGS

Juniper berries
(essential)
Coriander seeds
Caraway seeds
Orris root
Dried orange and lemon
peel
Angelica
Liquorice, fennel or
anise
Almonds
Cardamom pods

MIXING

Gin Smash: Dissolve a tablespoon of caster sugar in a little water, in a cocktail shaker. Add four large fresh mint sprigs and bruise, using a muddler to press the juices out of the mint. Half-fill the shaker with cracked ice and add two measures dry gin. Shake the cocktail vigorously for 20 seconds, then strain into a small glass filled with crushed ice and a little finely chopped mint.

advertiser today could get away with; the wording on one signboard famously ran: "*Drunk for a penny. Dead drunk for tuppence. Clean straw for nothing*". Such was the addiction of the masses to gin that it was actually made illegal by an Act of Parliament in 1736, but the law was hastily reversed six years later after it was predictably discovered that the contraband stuff that was now being drunk was considerably more toxic than the official spirit had been.

In 1750, the great social satirist William Hogarth produced his famous engraving *Gin Lane*. It depicted in minute detail the degradation and squalor that was being wrought by widespread consumption of gin. A century later, gin was still being blamed by critical commentators such as the author Charles Dickens as the corrosive solace of the destitute, although Dickens was more concerned to blame social inequity for the condition of the poor, rather than to see drink in itself as an evil. It was in this period, however, that the

great Temperance movements took root, and the poor were encouraged to fear drink as the devil's potion.

It was only in the late Victorian period that gin began to reassume a more dignified apparel. Because of its colourlessness and its absence of wood-derived richness, it was seen as a usefully ladylike alternative to Scotch whisky and cognac. The all-too-recent association with the sordid doings of the idle poor meant that some euphemism had to be found for it – a facility Victorian society was supremely practised in. For a while, it was improbably referred to as "white wine". Finally, the gin and tonic, the world's favourite aperitif, was born, and a new era in gin's fortunes was ushered in.

During the period of Prohibition in the United States (1919–33), gin became one of the more readily available sources of illicit hooch, largely because it was so

BEEFEATER
One of the most famous London gins

MIXING

Dry Martini: No cocktail recipe is more energetically argued over than the classic dry Martini. It is basically a generous measure of virtually neat stone-cold gin with a dash of dry white vermouth in it. But how much is a dash? Purists insist on no more than a single drop, or the residue left after briefly flushing the glass out with a splash of vermouth and then pouring it away. (They puzzlingly refer to such a Martini as "very dry", as if adding more vermouth would sweeten it. In fact, the terminology harks back to the original recipe, when the vermouth used was the sweet red variety.) Some go for as much as half a measure of vermouth, and I have at hand a book that suggests a two-to-one ratio of gin to vermouth – guaranteed to send the purist into paroxysms of horror. I have to admit I incline more to the purist philosophy, though: the vermouth should be added as if it were the last bottle in existence. The drink should properly be mixed gently in a separate jug, with ice, and then strained into the traditional cocktail glass (the real name of which is a martini glass). A twist of lemon peel should be squeezed delicately over the surface, so that the essential oil floats in globules on top of the drink, but *don't* put the lemon twist in the glass. And hold the olive. (Add a cocktail onion, however, and the drink becomes a **Gibson**.)

easy for amateur distillers to make. All that was needed was to add whatever flavourings you could lay your hands on to a basic grain spirit, and then bottle it as soon as you liked. It is sometimes said that a lot of the more outlandish cocktails of the Jazz Era owed their inspiration to the need to disguise the disgusting taste of home-made gin.

The reason that gin continues to provide the base for so many cocktails is that it is such a good mixer. Its lack of colour means that it doesn't turn an off-putting muddy hue when blended with fruit juices, as the brown spirits do, while its aromatic quality gives it something for the mixers to mingle with, as distinct from the absolute neutrality of vodka. Gin has inevitably lost a lot of ground to vodka in the more recent youth market, as its peculiar

PLYMOUTH GIN

Coates is the only producer of Plymouth gin.

BOOTH'S FINEST
Note that the company was established during the ban on gin in the UK

perfume is something of an acquired taste to untutored palates. In the 1990s, however, it suddenly found itself gaining new cachet among certain American rap artists, becoming the preferred tipple enthusiastically celebrated in their lyrics as "juice and gin" (in other words gin and orange, known to the Scott Fitzgerald set in the 1920s as Orange Blossom).

TYPES OF GIN

English Gin There are two types. London dry gin is by far the more commonly known, although it doesn't necessarily have to be distilled in the capital. It is an intensely perfumed spirit, and varies greatly in quality between producers. Gordon's, Booth's and Beefeater are the most famous names, but some speciality products have established a conspicuous presence on the market in recent years, notably Bombay Sapphire in the pale blue, tinted bottle.

HOW TO SERVE
Speciality gins can be served neat. Chill the bottle in the freezer, and serve the measures in small glasses. A taller, narrow-sided, stemmed glass – rather like a short champagne flute – is traditional in the Netherlands.

DUTCH GENEVER
The prototype
for London Gin

MIXING
Gin Swizzle: Beat together (as if you were preparing eggs for an omelette) a double measure of gin, a teaspoon of gomme (sugar syrup), the juice of a lime and a couple of firm dashes of Angostura in a large jug, with ice. When the drink is good and foaming, strain it into a tall glass. Alternatively, make the drink in the tall glass and stir it up with an old-fashioned swizzle stick.

The other type is Plymouth gin, of which there is only one distiller, Coates, at the Blackfriars distillery in the centre of the city, not far from the waterfront. Plymouth is a distinctly drier gin than the big London brands, its spirit is impressively rounded and the range of aromatics used in it somehow give it a subtler bouquet than most gin-drinkers may be used to. It makes an incomparable Pink Gin.

A very small amount of gin is cask-aged and referred to as golden gin after the colour it leaches out of the wood.

Dutch Genever This is quite a different drink to English gin, owing to the more pungently flavoured grain mash on which it is based. The mixture of barley, rye and corn is often quite heavily malted, giving the older spirits a lightly beery tinge in the colour. There are basically two grades, labelled either Oude (old) or Jonge (young), the latter looking more like the English article. They frequently come in an opaque "stone" bottle.

KIRSCH

KIRSCH IS THE ORIGINAL cherry spirit. It is a colourless pure distillate – a true brandy or eau de vie, in other words – made from cherries. It is included separately because it has traditionally been seen as a distinctive product from the other fruit brandies. A fair amount is made in the Alsace and Franche-Comté regions of eastern France, where they know a thing or two about such matters. It is also a particular speciality of the Schwarzwald, the Black Forest region of Bavaria in western Germany – hence its German name, which simply means "cherry". (Confusingly, Kirsch is not related to cherry brandy.)

When the cherry juice is pressed for the initial fermentation, the stones are ground up too and left to infuse in it. The stones impart a characteristic slightly bitter note to the spirit, and bequeath a minute and harmless amount of cyanide to it in the process. It is generally given a short period of ageing, but in large earthenware vats rather than barrels, so that it remains colourless. The true Kirsch cherry is the black Morello (the type that crops up in the Black Forest gâteau, Bavaria's gift to the world's

KIRSCH
A cherry eau de vie with an identity all of its own

OTHER NAMES
Germany: Kirschwasser, or Schwarzwalder

MIXING
Rose: Shake equal measures of Kirsch and dry vermouth with a dash of grenadine and plenty of ice. Strain into a cocktail glass.

dessert trolleys), but these days, red varieties are often used instead.

Kirsch is also made in Switzerland and Austria.

TASTES GOOD WITH
Use Kirsch to add a touch of alcoholic richness to desserts, whether for soaking the sponge base for a mousse, or moistening fresh fruit such as pineapple. Indeed, its flavour blends unexpectedly well with all sorts of fruits. Beware any bottle labelled "Kirsch de Cuisine". It is an inferior product, smelling more like candle-wax than cherries, whose roughness is supposedly disguised when used in cooking. And if you believe that…

HOW TO SERVE
Lightly chilled in small glasses, Kirsch makes a refreshing after-dinner tipple.

MARC

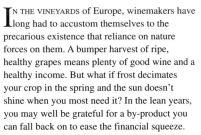

IN THE VINEYARDS of Europe, winemakers have long had to accustom themselves to the precarious existence that reliance on nature forces on them. A bumper harvest of ripe, healthy grapes means plenty of good wine and a healthy income. But what if frost decimates your crop in the spring and the sun doesn't shine when you most need it? In the lean years, you may well be grateful for a by-product you can fall back on to ease the financial squeeze.

For many thrifty wine producers, *marc* has traditionally been the answer. After the grape juice has been pressed for fermentation, a mass of smashed skins and pips, or pomace, is left, itself capable of fermentation. Marc is the distillate of this residue. In France, the most celebrated Marc is made in Burgundy and Champagne, frequently by producers enthusiastic enough to buy other growers' leftovers, but there is also some made in Alsace, Provence and the isolated eastern region of the Jura.

In Italy, Marc is known as grappa, and such is the connoisseurship surrounding it that varietal grappa, made from the skins of single grape varieties, has become

OTHER NAMES
Italy: grappa (also used in California)
Portugal: bagaceira
Spain: aguardiente (but that term may also be applied to any fiery grape spirit, including brandy)

something of a fad. An indication of its potential trendiness is that several producers in California (where the climate is sufficiently benign not to need such a stand-by) are making versions of grappa too. In all regions, the finer spirits may be treated to maturation in oak, resulting in a burnished golden colour, but most of it is clear.

TASTES GOOD WITH
I once ate a sorbet in Reims that had been made with Marc de Champagne, and anointed with yet more of it. It was acutely horrible, but in a somehow intriguing way. More beguiling is the use of Marc de Bourgogne for marinating the rind of the powerful local soft cheese of Chambertin.

HOW TO SERVE
Their strong tannins make marcs unsuitable for mixing. They are intended for drinking neat, though their profoundly earthy flavour may come as a shock to the uninitiated. On the calvados principle that a strong spirit aids digestion, the Burgundians in particular value them as after-dinner drinks.

GRAPPA
A varietal grappa made from Moscatel grapes

MARC DE CHAMPAGNE
Made by the champagne giants Moët & Chandon

MESCAL

ESCAL, OR MEZCAL, is one of Mexico's indigenous drinks. It is a pale yellowish spirit made from the juice of a species of cactus called the agave. The pressed juice is fermented to make *pulque*, a kind of beer of around 5–6% alcohol, which is known to have been consumed in Aztec times. It is then distilled once by the continuous method to produce mescal. (A second distillation removes more of the off-putting impurities in the spirit and results in the more highly prized tequila.)

It would be fair to say that mescal doesn't have a particularly illustrious image. It is the rapacious firewater that contributes to the downfall of the dissolute British

HOW TO SERVE

If the idea of chewing the worm as it is doesn't appeal, try liquidizing it in a cocktail. I have swallowed it in sections like aspirins, but the promised heroism – not surprisingly – failed to appear.

Consul in Malcolm Lowry's celebrated novel of alcoholism, *Under the Volcano*. In the past, it was considered to be capable of inducing gruesome hallucinations, a feature Lowry's novel reports, but it is hard to account for this since the agave cactus – or American aloe, as it is sometimes known – is not one of the hallucinogenic species.

Mescal is often sold with a pickled white agave worm in the bottle. It is genuine, and is intended to be eaten as the last of the drink is poured out. Supposedly, ingestion of the worm encourages great heroism in those already brave enough to swallow it. Again, the myth persists that the worm, which feeds on the agave plant, contains hallucinogenic properties. If that is likely to be your only motivation for trying it, don't bother. (The psychedelic drug, mescaline, was derived from the peyote cactus, not the agave.)

HOW IT IS MADE

The unlovely agave plant has an enormous core, the shape of a pine-cone, which is surrounded by great, spiny fat leaves. This core, or heart, is hacked away and the expressed juice – which is milky-white and extremely bitter – is fermented into pulque. Mescal is the first rough distillation of the pulque. It may be given a short period of ageing in wood, but it is not intended to be a sophisticated product.

TASTES GOOD WITH

Agave worm.

MESCAL
A little white worm
lurks at the bottom
of every bottle

HOW TO SERVE

If you want to tame its fire, try mixing mescal with a little freshly squeezed lime juice and topping it up with soda or tonic water. In Mexico, inevitably, they just knock it back as it is, like schnapps. It is hard to find a mescal, even commercially bottled, that doesn't smell dirty, an aroma that does tend to pierce through whatever it's mixed with.

RUM

RUM IS PROBABLY the least understood of the five main spirits, despite the fact that, in its white version, it is one of the biggest-selling of them all. Indeed, it is debatable whether many of those knocking back Bacardi-and-Cokes in bars around the world realize they are drinking some form of rum at all. In the popular mind, the drink is inextricably associated with a rather antiquated pantomime idea of "Jolly Jack Tars" and a life on the ocean wave.

There is some uncertainty over the origin of the spirit's name, but the favourite theory is that it is a shortening of a rather marvellous old West Country English word "rumbullion", itself of unknown origin, but generally denoting any hard liquor.

The invention of rum probably dates from not long after the foundation of the sugar plantations in the West Indies, in the early 16th century. Until the voyages of Christopher Columbus, sugar was a luxury product, and much sought after in southern Europe, having originally been brought from India into Venice by Persians and then by Arabs. When the Spanish explorers landed in Hispaniola (modern-day Haiti and the Dominican Republic) and the neighbouring Caribbean islands, they saw in them promising environments for cultivating sugar cane and thereby breaking the stranglehold on the market that the Arabs had.

If yeasts need sugar to feed on in order to produce alcohol, then the sugar plant was always going to be an obvious source for some kind of distillate. When first pressed,

OTHER NAMES
France: rhum
Spain: ron

HOW TO SERVE
The best dark rums, and aged rums in particular, should be served straight, unchilled, as digestifs. They make stimulating alternatives to malt whisky or cognac. Premium white rums from the independent producers are also best enjoyed neat, but they should be served cold.

NOTABLE PRODUCERS
Appleton, Myers (Jamaica);
CSR (St Kitts);
Green Island (Mauritius);
Clément, Rhum St James, La Mauny (Martinique);
Havana Club (Cuba);
El Dorado (Guyana);
Cockspur, Mount Gay (Barbados);
Barbancourt (Haiti);
Pusser's (British Virgin Islands)

CAPTAIN MORGAN
The leading brand dark rum

Rum is the base for many of the more
way-out cocktail concoctions on offer today,
its heady richness contributing to the explo-
sive power required. Here are two classics:
Bacardi Cocktail: The original, after which
the brand is named. Shake a double
measure of white rum with the juice of half a
lime, a teaspoon of grenadine, and ice. Strain
it into a cocktail glass.
Cuba Libre (below): Mix a generous
measure of light or golden rum with a tablespoon or so of freshly squeezed lime juice,
pour over ice, and top up with cola.

cane juice is a murky, greenish colour and full
of impurities. Boiled down, it eventually crys-
tallizes into sucrose and a sticky, brown
by-product, molasses, that would readily have
fermented in the tropical conditions. Rum is the
spirit derived from distilling the fermented
molasses.

Sugar soon became a widespread everyday
product in Europe. The astronomical demand
for it was serviced by one of the most notorious
manifestations of European colonial history –
the slave trade – and rum played a crucial part
in the circular trade that came to be established.
Settlers in New England financed their trips to
West Africa by selling rum. A consignment of
African slaves would be delivered to the West

Indies and sold for molasses, which would then
be shipped back to New England to be turned
into more rum.

The association of rum with the British Navy
in particular derives from the fact that rum was
provided to the ratings as a standard daily
ration in the 18th century. The tradition continued throughout the most glorious period of
Britain's maritime
history, basically
because rum could
withstand hot weather
more sturdily than beer
could. The initial
allowance was a fairly
rollicking half-pint a
day, which eventually
was watered down into
the despised "grog"

WOOD'S 100
*A particularly rich
naval-strength
dark rum*

Petite Fleur: (from
Michael Walker's
*Cinzano Cocktail
Book*): Shake equal
measures of white
rum, Cointreau and
freshly squeezed
grapefruit juice with
ice and strain into a
cocktail glass.
Mai Tai (below):
Blend a measure each
of dark rum and light
rum with half-
measures of tequila,
Cointreau and apricot
brandy, a measure of
freshly squeezed
orange juice, a splash
of grenadine and a few
drops of Angostura and
ice cubes in a
liquidizer. Decant into
a very large wine
glass. Approach with
trepidation.

MIXING

Planter's Punch: Shake a double measure each of light rum and fresh orange juice with a couple of teaspoons of fresh lemon juice and ice, and strain into a large glass. (Some authorities insist on a dash of grenadine just for good measure.)

Ti Punch (below): Stir a generous measure of good white rum with a splash of cane syrup and the pounded zest and juice of a lime in a large tumbler with plenty of crushed ice. (Not to be confused with tea punch, which is actually based on tea.)

HOW TO SERVE

Of the commercial products, white rum mixes famously well with cola, but also with orange juice or more tropical flavours such as pineapple or mango. Dark rum has traditionally been seen as compatible with blackcurrant or peppermint cordials, as well as the ubiquitous cola (below).

growing sugar cane specifically for distillation.

Some rum is made from the pressed cane juice itself, but most is made from the fermented molasses. In the former French colonies in particular, there is a distinguished tradition of *rhum agricole*, speciality products made on small sugar farms, in which rums are produced with different strains of yeast. They are individually appreciated in the same way that a wine drinker appreciates wines made from single grape varieties.

Both methods of distillation are practised for rum

and then mixed with lemon juice as an antiscorbutic (but it was still not much less than a third of a pint of spirit). It was only as recently as 1970 that it was decided that perhaps encouraging the lads to drink around eight measures of spirit every day might not be the best guarantee of military efficiency.

Rum is today produced all over the West Indies and eastern South America, to a lesser extent in the Indian Ocean area – the Philippines and Mauritius – and in smaller quantities still in the United States and even in Australia. A lot of it is inevitably a by-product of the sugar-refining industry, but the best grades are made by smaller, independent companies

BACARDI
The world's favourite white spirit brand

MIXING

Hot Buttered Rum: In a tall glass, mix a teaspoon of demerara sugar in a good double measure of strong black rum. Add half a teaspoon of ground cinnamon and a knob of unsalted butter and fill with hot water. (Remember to stand a spoon in the glass to conduct the heat if the water has just boiled.) Stir well to dissolve the butter and sugar.

Pina Colada (below): Whizz up two measures each of white rum and pineapple juice, with a couple of teaspoons of shredded fresh coconut and ice, in a liquidizer. (For that tropical touch, the drink should ideally be poured into a pineapple shell with a good lining of fruit left in it and drunk through straws.)

important category commercially, and it is certainly where the superior products are found. Leading brands are Captain Morgan and Lamb's, but there are many others. Some of them are bottled at the original naval strength of more than 50% ABV (Wood's Navy Rum, for example, is 57%), the traditional name for which was "overproof". The everyday dark rums are a more standard 40%, while Bacardi is adjusted down to 37.5% to put it on a level with the other commercial white spirits.

In between the two styles is the increasingly

MOUNT GAY BARBADOS
A major Caribbean brand of golden rum

and, as with other spirits, the premium versions are double-distilled in a copper pot still. Continuous distillation and thorough rectification are used mainly by the bulk producers, particularly for the relatively neutral-tasting white rums that lead the market. Freshly distilled spirit from the pot still method is very high in impurities and must be allowed to mellow through a period of cask-ageing, which in turn gives colour to the darker rums. Some companies adjust the final colour with caramel, but not to a degree that would affect the flavour.

After white rums, dark rum is the next most

MIXING

Daiquiri: Shake a double measure of white rum with the juice of half a lime or a quarter of a lemon, a teaspoon of caster sugar and ice. Strain into a cocktail glass. (Adding half a measure of some fruit liqueur, together with 50g/2oz of the equivalent fresh fruit, puréed, is a popular spin on the original Daiquiri. A strawberry version made with fraise liqueur is especially enticing.)

FLAVOURINGS

A small amount of rum is aromatized with mixed spices and fruits such as raisins and plums. Some of Guyana's Demerara rums are flavoured in this way

MIXING

Zombie: Blend a measure each of dark rum, light rum and apricot brandy with half-measures of pineapple juice and freshly squeezed lemon and orange juices in a liquidizer, with ice, and pour into a large goblet.

of the residue of the first distillation – known as dunder – may be added to the molasses during fermentation. Commercial white rums are rectified and bottled immediately. Coloured rums are cask-aged, sometimes for decades, before they are bottled.

TASTES GOOD WITH

More than any other basic spirit, rum makes an excellent accompaniment to fruits of all kinds. A "salad" of orange segments in golden rum was already a traditional dish in the 18th century. Rum can be added to the syrup for all fruit salads, though, and works particularly well with pineapple and banana. It is excellent for adding an enriching note to sponge-based desserts such as charlottes. Rum baba – the soft sponge filled with raisins and soaked in light rum – would, of course, be nothing without it.

popular golden or light rum, which is a particular speciality of Cuba and Puerto Rico aged for less time in barrel. The darkest and heaviest rums, some not far from the colour of thick black treacle, traditionally come from Jamaica. Good white rum, such as the white Rhum St James from Martinique, is full of burnt-sugar richness, a world away from the blandness of commercial white. Some exporters make a virtue of selling rums with 30 or 40 years of cask age, and there is even a tiny production of vintage-dated rum for the true connoisseur.

HOW IT IS MADE

Juice from the sugar cane is pressed and either fermented straight, or else boiled down to extract the molasses, which itself forms the basis of the ferment. It is either continuously distilled or, for speciality products, double-distilled in a pot still. For a headier product, some

LAMB'S
One of the leading brands of dark rum

SLIVOVITZ

TRUE SLIVOVITZ IS, or was, the local fruit brandy, or eau de vie, of Serbia and Bosnia-Herzegovina. I say "was" because the ravages of the war in the early 1990s in the former Yugoslavia, of which those countries were once part, put paid to a lot of the production capacity of the distilleries. Indeed it put paid to whole distilleries in some cases. A little did continue to be made, however (its rarity value leading one London retailer at the time to triple the price of its remaining stocks), and with peace production may rise once more.

It is to be hoped so because, at its best, slivovitz is one of the most distinguished and delicious eaux de vie made anywhere in Europe. The base fruit is a particular variety of black plum called Madjarka, which imparts a richly heady scent to the spirit. For the best grades, the spirit is cask-aged, and steeped in yet more whole fresh fruit during maturation to emphasize the flavour. It comes in a variety of weirdly shaped bottles, some tall and thin, some round and flask-shaped, still others of faceted glass.

Slivovitz has always been made and drunk elsewhere in eastern and central Europe, notably Bulgaria, Hungary, Germany, Austria and Italy. In the Balkans, it may also go by its other name of *rakija*. This name denotes its origin as one of the European fruit versions of the arak that came from the Far East.

HOW IT IS MADE

Black plums are crushed along with their stones and fermented very slowly over a period of around three months. A double distillation is carried out, and then the new spirit is aged in great casks of Slovenian oak. Sometimes, whole plums are thrown in to macerate in the spirit while it ages. It is generally bottled at about five years old and at 35–40% ABV.

TASTES GOOD WITH

A little slivovitz added to stewed plums, or even to a traditional Christmas pudding, will enrich the dish no end.

SLIVOVITZ
is heady with the
scent of ripe black
plums

OTHER NAMES
Bosnia, Croatia,
Serbia: sljivovica. Also
rakija/prakija/slivovka

SLJIVOVICA
A Croatian
slivovitz in a
flask-shaped
bottle

HOW TO SERVE
As with all such spirits, slivovitz is most commonly drunk unchilled, as a digestif.

TEQUILA

TEQUILA IS THE NATIONAL spirit of Mexico. It is one stage further down the road to refinement than its fellow cactus-based spirit, mescal, but several leagues ahead in terms of drinking pleasure. It starts life as *pulque*, the fermented beer-like juice of the agave plant, and is distilled twice before being aged in cask. It comes in two versions, clear like vodka, and golden (or Oro), which spends a longer period in contact with the barrels. Virtually unknown in Europe until comparatively recently, it made its first inroads into the world's drinks cabinet by travelling north-wards to the USA, and it is now something of a cult drink in the youth market.

The name, tequila, is echoed in the full botanical name of the

JOSE CUERVO

Fundada en 1795

Tequila

HECHO EN MEXICO

70 cl ℮   PRODUCE OF MEXICO   38% vol

CUERVO TEQUILA
The white version of Mexico's national spirit

MIXING
Tequila and Orange: Have done with the fuss, and drink it on the rocks with fresh orange juice. It makes an enlivening change for those grown weary of vodka-and-orange.

HOW TO SERVE
The correct way of drinking tequila: your drink is served to you cold and straight in a small shot-glass. You then season your tongue with citrus and salt, by first squeezing a wedge of lime (lemon for the wimps) and then pouring salt on to the back of the hand and licking at each in turn. To be anatomically precise, the hand should be held at a 45° angle away from the body, with the thumb extended downwards, and the juice and salt deposited along the groove between the bases of the thumb and forefinger. (Some make things easier by just sucking on the piece of lime.) The tequila is then thrown back in one gulp like schnapps, carrying the seasonings with it. The process is repeated ad infinitum.

Believe it or not, this really is how tequila is widely drunk on its native territory. If it sounds like a fiddly and indescribably messy procedure, the answer is that it is, but long practice induces a sort of head-tossing, devil-may-care sanguinity in experienced users.

MIXING

Margarita: Shake equal measures of tequila and Cointreau with the juice of half a lime and plenty of ice. Dip a finger in and run it around the rim of a cocktail glass. Up-end the glass briefly in a saucerful of coarse-ground salt, then strain the drink into it. (This is the classic tequila cocktail, but it is just a customized way of getting round the traditional salt-licking routine – with a slug of Cointreau for sweetly counteracting the salt. Some recipes add egg white too. No accounting for taste.)

HOW IT IS MADE

Like mescal, tequila is distilled from the chopped, pressed and fermented hearts of agave plants. The juice is quite high in acidity, which lends even the refined spirit a certain piquancy. It is distilled a second time in a pot still, and then matured in wooden casks, briefly for the white version, and up to five years for the Oro.

*GOLDEN
MONTEZUMA*
*Gold tequila has
aged in cask for
longer than white*

MIXING
Tequila Sunrise: Half-fill a tall glass with crushed ice. Put in a goodly measure of tequila and top up with fresh orange juice. Quickly dollop a teaspoon of grenadine into the centre of the drink. (The bright red grenadine sinks to the bottom and then blends upwards into the orange in a very becoming way, hence the drink's name.)

plant from which it is sourced: *Agave tequilana*. Perhaps what put everybody else off trying it for so long was the thought of a spirit made from cacti, and indeed even the finest grades don't actually smell particularly inviting. It has a sweaty, slightly muggy quality that must have come as something of a jolt at first to tastebuds honed on squeaky-clean vodka.

In recognition of its cultural importance, the production of tequila has been strictly delimited within Mexico. It may be distilled in only a handful of towns, including Tequila itself, and in the area immediately surrounding Guadalajara. Two of the brands most commonly encountered on the export markets are Cuervo and Montezuma, the latter usually in an engraved bottle.

VODKA

IN ONE SENSE, vodka is the closest thing to perfection ever conceived in the long history of spirits. Had it been invented in the 1990s, in the era of alco-pops and ice beers, it would be hailed as a supremely adept piece of marketing wizardry. Nobody, other than a confirmed teetotaller, could possibly dislike it, for the simple reason that it tastes of nothing whatsoever. It is pure, unadulterated, uncomplicated alcohol. At least, most of it is.

The word "vodka" is a Russian endearment meaning "little water", from their word for water, *voda*. It doesn't denote the flavourlessness of the spirit, however, but derives from the widespread linguistic practice in Europe of referring to all distillates originally as a form of water (as in the Latin *aqua vitae* and French *eau de vie*).

Precisely because it is such a simple drink, it is almost impossible to pinpoint the origins of vodka historically. A potent spirit distilled from various grains, and

indeed potatoes – still wrongly believed in the popular imagination to be its main ingredient – has been made in Poland, Russia and the Baltic states of Latvia, Lithuania and Estonia since the very early days of distillation in Europe.

But as to where a drink specifically recognizable as vodka first arose is a matter for the Poles and the Russians to sort out between themselves. (Most outsiders, it should be said, tend to come down on the Polish side of the fence these days.) What is certain is that, by the time home distillation had become a favoured way of passing the long, grim northern winters in Poland, peasant families were producing their own vodkas on an extensive scale.

The discovery of rectification

HOW TO SERVE
Everything should be almost painfully cold. The bottle should be kept in the freezer and the glasses too should be iced. If there isn't a heavy mist of condensation on the outside of the glass, it isn't cold enough.

Some shots are thrown back like schnapps, owing to an old folk belief that if you inhale the fumes for more than a split second, you will get too drunk too quickly. The aged vodkas, and specialities such as Zubrowka, are more often sipped appreciatively. A little shot-glass is traditional, but in some homes, a rather larger, narrow tumbler, or even something like a goblet wine glass is used.

SMIRNOFF
The basic red label brand is the market leader

ABSOLUT
Blue label Absolut is the unflavoured version

techniques did not take place until the beginning of the 19th century, and so these early distillates would have tasted pretty unclean, to say the least. Any herbs, seeds or berries that were to hand would be steeped in the spirit to mask its rankness. So the first vodkas were not the anonymous products preferred today, but the true ancestors of the flavoured vodkas that are sometimes greeted as nothing more than novelty items by modern drinkers.

Nonetheless, it was the neutral, ultra-purified grain vodka – made from wheat or rye – that came to commercial prominence in the West. So prevalent is it now, particularly among younger drinkers who have yet to discover and appreciate the taste of unrectified, cask-matured spirits such as good whisky and cognac, that it is hard to believe that hardly anyone in western Europe or America had heard of it until the late 1940s.

BLACK LABEL SMIRNOFF
A softer, mellower product

BLUE LABEL SMIRNOFF
The strongest at 45%

MIXING

Basic vodka has no scent or flavour, meaning it is not the most inspiring ingredient in the cocktail repertoire. All it can really do is confer an extra slug of alcohol for those hell-bent on the short-cut to oblivion. As a result, the sky's the limit.
Black Russian: The true Black Russian is simply equal measures of vodka and Tia Maria, or Kahlúa, mixed with ice cubes in a tumbler. However, the fashion in recent years has been to serve it as a long drink in a big glass, topped up with cola. Alternatively, leave out the cola, add a measure of single cream, shake it up and it becomes a
White Russian: Then again, substitute dark brown crème de cacao for the Tia Maria and create a **Piranha**.
Black Cossack (below): Add a good slug of vodka to a half-pint of Guinness.

FLAVOURINGS

Vodka will happily take up whatever flavouring a producer decides to give it, including:
Lemon peel
Bison grass
Red chilli peppers
Cherries
Rowanberries
Blackcurrants
Apples
Sloes
Saffron
Tarragon
Walnuts
Honey
Liquorice
Rose petals

It all changed with the first stirrings of interest in California during the period of the Beat Generation.

Not only did vodka possess the aforementioned neutrality that made it such an obvious beginner's spirit, but it was also seen as a provocatively dissident thing to drink in the era of the onset of the Cold War. Vodka was the favoured "hooch" of the Soviet bloc, and in the witch-hunting atmosphere of 50s America, nothing was more guaranteed to inflame bourbon-drinking patriots than to see young folks imbibing the spirit of Communism with such evident glee. The late Alexis Lichine,

LIMONNAYA
A leading lemon-
flavoured vodka

drink historian, attributes the start of vodka's meteoric rise in the West to the purchase of a recipe for rectified vodka from a Russian refugee called Smirnoff by an American company, on the eve of the Second World War. The rest is history.

Vodka is still very much the drink of gastronomic choice in its native lands, drunk as aperitif, digestif and even as an accompaniment to food. It is nearly always taken icy-cold, preceded in Polish homes by the ritual wishing of good health – *na zdrowie* – to one's family and friends. The quantities consumed may raise eyebrows in our Western unit-counting culture, but a vodka hangover is very rare, owing to the relentless clean-up job the drink is given during distillation. This removes nearly all of its congeners, the substances that impart character to the dark spirits.

Fruit flavourings are very common, and make a drier, more bracing alternative to the equivalent liqueurs. Perhaps the most celebrated flavoured product is Zubrowka, bison-grass vodka, which is generally sold with a

MIXING

Screwdriver: That nightclub favourite, vodka and orange. The name, according to one theory, originated among workers on American oil-rigs who – finding themselves short of swizzle-sticks – resourcefully used their screwdrivers to stir the drink. In the Baltic states, the freshly squeezed orange juice is served to you in a separate little jug and you mix to taste. Even here the cocktail name is in use, although, as I discovered in Riga, to make yourself perfectly clear, you must ask the barman for a "skrew". When first marketed on the west coast of the USA, it was suggested that it be drunk with ginger beer. Thus did the first **Moscow Mule** come to light.

ABSOLUT
Kurant is
solidly fruity
and flavoured
with black-
currants

MIXING

Bloody Mary: Everyone has his or her own proprietary recipe for the next best hangover cure after aspirin. Some strange people even put tomato ketchup into it. Others round out the alcohol with a splash of dry sherry. Here is my own formula.

Put a slice of lemon and two or three ice-cubes in a tall glass, add a teaspoon of Lea & Perrin's Worcestershire sauce, a teaspoon of freshly squeezed lemon juice, a pinch of celery salt, a generous dash of Tabasco and about half-a-dozen twists of the black pepper mill, and stir to coat the ice. Fill the glass to about an inch-and-a-half from the top with tomato juice and pour on a generous measure of vodka. Stir well to combine the alcohol.

blade of grass in the bottle. Bison grass is the gourmet preference of the wild bison that roam the forests of eastern Poland, and the beast is usually depicted on the label.

Wisniowka (cherries), Limonnaya (lemon) and the Swedish Absolut company's Kurant (blackcurrant) are all appetizing drinks. Pieprzowka, which is infused with chilli peppers, is a variety for real aficionados: the spirit is emphasized by the hot spice burn of its flavouring component. Russia's Okhotnichya – "Hunter's Vodka" – is impregnated with orange peel, ginger root, coffee beans, juniper berries and even a drop of white port.

Neutral vodkas are produced all over the

world now, although most grades are only intended to be served in mixed drinks. Russian Stolichnaya, particularly the Cristall bottling, is an honourable, silky-smooth exception. Smirnoff makes three types, in red, blue and black labels to denote varying strength, and there are brands with such names as Black Death and Jazz Jamboree. Scandinavian vodkas such as Finlandia and Absolut have their deserved followings, while most British vodka tends to be little more than patent alcohol. At one time, vodka production had even travelled south from Russia into Iran, but the coming of Islamic rule brought that to a halt.

Also seen on the export markets is Polish Pure Spirit, bottled at around 70% ABV, and much beloved by reckless students as a dare.

HOW IT IS MADE

Although potatoes and other vegetables, and even molasses, have been used to make vodka at various times in its history, commercial vodka is nowadays virtually exclusively made from grains, the principal one of which is rye. A basic mash is made in the usual way by malting the grains and encouraging them to ferment with cultured yeasts. The resulting brew is then continuously

PIEPRZOWKA
This vodka has been coloured and flavoured with chillies

distilled in a column still apparatus to higher and higher degrees of alcoholic strength, thus driving off nearly all of the higher alcohols or fusel oil. As a final insurance policy against flavour, the finished spirit is then filtered through a layer of charcoal, which strips it of any remaining character. It is then bottled at around 37.5% for commercial strength and released without further ado.

In the case of flavoured vodkas, the aromatizing elements are added to the new spirit after rectification, and left to infuse in it over long periods – sometimes three years or more. Occasionally, a speciality vodka will be aged in cask and take on a tinge of colour; others derive their exotic hues from the addition of spices, flowers or nuts.

TASTES GOOD WITH

Ice-cold vodka is the classic accompaniment to finest Russian caviare, itself served on heaps of ice. In the Scandinavian countries, it is also drunk, like aquavit, with marinated and smoked fish such as herring, mackerel and even salmon. Superchef Martin Blunos at Restaurant Lettonie, near Bristol in England, has created a sumptuously theatrical dish of scrambled duck egg served in the shell amid a slick of flaming Latvian vodka, topped with sevruga caviare and with blinis and a shot of freezing vodka on the side.

STOLICHNAYA
This smooth vodka should be sipped appreciatively

MIXING

Balalaika: Shake a measure each of vodka and Cointreau with half a measure of lemon juice and plenty of ice, and strain into a cocktail glass.

Barbara: Shake a measure of vodka with half-measures of crème de cacao and single cream, with ice, and strain into a cocktail glass. (This is essentially a vodka-based **Alexander**.)

Katinka (from Michael Walker's *Cinzano Cocktail Book*): Shake a measure-and-a-half of vodka with a measure of apricot brandy and half a measure of fresh lime juice with ice, and pour over a heap of slivered ice in a cocktail glass.

Vodkatini: Basically a classic Martini, but with vodka replacing the gin.

Czarina: Stir a measure of vodka with half-measures of apricot brandy and dry vermouth and a dash of Angostura with ice in a mixing jug. Strain into a cocktail glass.

WHISKY

WHISKY (OR WHISKEY, depending on where it hails from) is one of the world's leading spirits. Its history is every bit as distinguished as that of cognac and, like the classic brandies of France, its spread around the world from its first home – the Scottish Highlands, in whisky's case – has been a true testament to the genius of its conception. Tennessee sour mash may bear about as much relation in taste to single malt Scotch as Spanish brandy does to cognac, but the fact that they are all great products demonstrates the versatility of each basic formula.

Whiskies are produced all over the world now. As the name is not a geographically specific one, they may all legitimately call themselves whisk(e)y. In Australia and India, the Czech Republic and Germany, they make grain spirits from barley or rye that proudly bear the name. The five major whisky-producing countries are Scotland, the United States, Ireland, Canada and Japan, which are covered in this chapter.

The name "whisky" itself is yet another variant on the phrase "water of life" that we have become familiar with in the world of spirits. In translation, the Latin *aqua vitae* became *uisge beatha* in the Scots branch of Gaelic and *usque-baugh* in the Irish; it eventually was mangled into the half-Anglicized "whisky"

and was in official use by the mid-18th century.

In countries that lacked the warm climate for producing fermented drinks from grapes, beer was always the staple brew and, just as brandy was the obvious first distillate in southern Europe, so malted grains provided the starting-point for domestic production further north. Unlike brandy, however, which starts life as wine, whisky doesn't have to be made from something that would be recognizable as beer. The grains are malted by allowing them to germinate in water and then lightly cooking them to encourage the formation of sugars. It is these sugars on which the yeasts then feed to produce the first ferment. A double distillation by the pot still method results in a congener-rich

MACALLAN
This 18-year-old whisky is one of the best-loved Highland malts

LAPHROAIG
One of the richest of the peaty styles of Scotch produced in Islay

HOW TO SERVE

The finest whiskies are not necessarily drunk neat. It is widely believed that taming some of the spirit's fire helps to bring up the array of complicated scents and flavours in good whisky. To that end, it is normally drunk with a dose of water, ideally the same spring water that goes into the whisky itself, otherwise any pure, non-chlorinated water. Half-and-half are the preferred proportions in Scotland and Ireland, while in Tennessee and Kentucky they add a little less than half.

spirit that can then be matured – often for decades for the finer whiskies – in oak barrels.

Just as with other spirits that haven't had the life rectified out of them, whisky is nearly always truly expressive of its regional origins and the raw materials that went into it. For that reason, a passionate connoisseurship of this spirit has arisen over the generations, similar to that which surrounds wine. Even more than brandy, whisky handsomely rewards those who set out with a conscientious approach to the tasting and appreciation of the spirit.

SCOTLAND

Home distillation in Scotland can be traced back to the 15th century, when the practice of distilling surplus grain to make a potent drink for clan chieftains was established. Initially, the drink was – like all spirits – primarily valued

for its medicinal powers, and early examples were no doubt infusions of herbs and berries rather than the pure grain product we know today. Although other cereals would at first have been used, the pre-eminence of malted barley was acknowledged relatively early on in the development of Scotch.

Before the Act of Union that brought England and Scotland together politically in 1707, Scotch was hardly known in England. Gin was the national drink south of the border. Once the English laid their administrative hands on Scotland, they did their level best to bring whisky distillation under statutory control, but with only very partial success. Those whisky-makers within striking distance of the border fled northwards with their stills into the Highlands, and the production of Scotch continued unabated as an almost wholly illicit activity.

Eventually, by a combination of threats and bribes, the authorities managed to place the whole enterprise under licence so that, by the 1870s, there

GLENLIVET
A 10-year-old Spey-side malt from the Scottish Highlands

TASTES GOOD WITH
Scotch is naturally the only accompaniment to the ceremonial haggis on Burns Night (January 25). Whether it is a precise gastronomic match may be open to question, but to order a bottle of Rioja would be missing the point somewhat. Un-iced Scotch is also great with hearty soups: thick, barley-based Scotch broth or cock-a-leekie should ideally have a fair amount of whisky in them anyway.

TALISKER
Talisker whisky is the only malt whisky produced on the island of Skye.

MIXING
Rusty Nail: Equal
measures of Scotch and
Drambuie mixed with
ice and strained into a
small glass, or poured
over crushed ice.
Whisky Mac (below):
The classic cold
remedy is half and half
good Scotch and green
ginger wine
(preferably Crabbie's)
with no ice.

were just half-a-dozen arraignments in Scotland for illegal distilling (as against nearly 700 only 40 years earlier).

The advent of continuous distillation came to Scotland courtesy of Robert Stein, who invented a rudimentary version of the column still in 1826. Although Scotch had traditionally been characterized by the richness and depth of flavour that marks all pot-still products, the development of the new method allowed a lighter spirit of more obvious commercial appeal to be produced. By the late 19th century, the habit of blending true malt whisky with straight grain spirit made by continuous distillation from unmalted barley (and maize, or corn) was widespread. These were the types of Scotch that were introduced to cautious English palates.

In the early years of this century, a Royal Commission was set up to determine the parameters for Scotch whisky production, i.e. the methods of distillation, rules on blending, minimum maturation times and, of course, the salient geographical point – that Scotch could only be distilled and aged in Scotland. The Commission reported in 1909, its conclusions were refined slightly in 1915, and it remains in force today as the legal textbook for an industry of worldwide importance that is also a central support of the Scottish economy.

THE FAMOUS
GROUSE
One of the
leading brands
of blended Scotch

TYPES OF SCOTCH
The most highly prized of Scotch whiskies are the single malts. These are whiskies that are produced entirely from malted barley, double-distilled, and made exclusively at a single one (hence the terminology) of Scotland's 100 or so working distilleries. Some of these products are aged for many years. Twenty-five-year-old Scotch will be shot through with all sorts of profoundly complex flavours and perfumes picked up from the wood in which it has matured and perhaps, according to some, from the sea air that wafts around the coastal distilleries. Remember that – as with other spirits – aged malt can't continue to develop once bottled.

Some malts are the blended produce of several single malts, in which case they are known as vatted malts. They are often assembled from several distilleries within a particular region in order to illustrate the local style comparable to specific regional subdivisions in a *vin de pays* wine area.

Whiskies made from corn or unmalted barley are known as grain whiskies and are always considerably

WHYTE &
MACKAY
This whisky is
re-blended for a
second period
of maturation

lighter in style than the malts. They could be described as beginner's Scotch since they have far fewer of the aromatic components that account for the pedigree of great malt, but they should by no means be seen as worthless imitations. They have their role to play.

The greater part of that role is in the production of blended Scotch, whisky made from a mixture of malt and grain spirits. This is the market-leading category, occupied by virtually all of the big brand names, such as Bell's, J&B, Johnnie Walker, Ballantine's, Whyte & Mackay, The Famous Grouse, White Horse and Teacher's. Most of these have fairly low concentrations of malt in the blend, although Teacher's and Johnnie Walker's Black Label

J&B
This blended whisky is popular in the American market; J&B stands for Justerini & Brooks

bottling are notable exceptions.

Scotch whisky is mostly retailed at the standard dark spirit strength of 40% ABV, or perhaps slightly above (avoid any that are below). A small proportion of the best grades are bottled from the barrel undiluted. These are known as "cask-strength" whiskies. You are not intended to drink them as they come, but the distiller is inviting you to dilute them with water yourself and find the precise level of potency that suits you.

AREAS OF PRODUCTION

For the purposes of whisky production, Scotland is divided up into four broad regions: the Lowlands, south of Stirling; the tiny Campbeltown, on a narrow peninsula west of Ayr; Islay and the Western

GLENMORANGIE
One of the most celebrated Northern Highland malts.

TEACHERS
One of the maltier blended whiskies.

GIFT WRAPPING
Malt whiskies are often sold in elegant presentation cartons.

Isles, comprising Jura, Mull and Skye; and the Highlands. The Highlands can be further sub-divided into the Midlands, the Western, Northern and Eastern Highlands and Speyside.

As a (very) rough guide to the regional styles, Lowland whiskies are the gentlest and sweetest styles of Scotch, while Campbeltown's are fresh and ozoney. Islay produces an instantly recognizable pungent spirit, full of seaweed aromas, and particularly marked by the influence of the peat that fires the drying kilns for the grain, while many Highland malts have a soft smokiness to them. There are numerous distilleries, though, and each has evolved its own style.

HOW IT IS MADE

In the case of the malts, the grains of barley are soaked in water to encourage them to germinate. Soon after they have begun sprouting, the process is arrested by heating them in a kiln, in which variable quantities of peat will be added to the fuel, depending on

the intended final flavour of the whisky. After kilning, the grain is mashed and drained and then poured into large tanks to begin fermentation, either with natural or cultured yeasts. (Yeast strains have a pronounced effect on the flavour, too.) The resulting brew is then double-distilled in the traditional copper pot still.

The other factor of huge significance in determining the character of a whisky is the type of maturation vessel. Scotch was traditionally aged in casks that had previously been used for shipping sherry, and some still is, but used bourbon casks from Kentucky are now quite common. In both cases, the wood is American oak, capable of imparting great richness to a whisky. (There is at least one product on the market that has been aged in old port casks.) Whiskies aged for long periods will derive a certain character from the action of oxygen seeping through the pores of the wood.

WHITE HORSE
A pronounced
peatiness marks
the flavour of
this blended
whisky

JOHNNIE WALKER
Red Label is the biggest selling whisky of all.

JOHNNIE WALKER
The Black Label has a higher malt content than the red

UNITED STATES

In North America, where whiskey is mostly spelled with an "e" as it is in Ireland, production of the drink goes back only as far as the 18th century. Its roots are embedded in the era leading up to Independence. Before that, the staple spirit in America was dark rum, made from molasses transported from the West Indies by the slave ships. It was British and Irish settlers, bringing their own whisky with them from the old countries, who provided the impetus for the development of what is today America's national spirit.

The first American whiskeys were made with malted barley and rye, in vague imitation of the European archetypes. Soon, however, a group of distillers in Bourbon County, Kentucky, began producing pure corn whiskey. By happy chance, their little communities were descended upon from 1794 onwards by droves of tax refugees who were fleeing from revenue officers in Pennsylvania, after staging an armed uprising against the new State excises on liquor. Suddenly, the Kentuckians had a ready-made new market for their own product and, before

too long, Kentucky bourbon was well on its way to assuming a place in the ranks of the world's fine spirits.

Rye whiskey is still made in the eastern states of Pennsylvania, Maryland and Virginia, but seemingly in ever-decreasing quantities. It is the whiskeys of Kentucky and Tennessee that represent the cognac and armagnac, if you will, of American spirit production.

BOURBON

Nowadays, most bourbon distilleries are concentrated not in Bourbon County, but around the towns of Louisville, Bardstown and Frankfort. Nonetheless, only whiskeys from the state of Kentucky are entitled to be called bourbons. Bourbon is not a straight corn whiskey, but one made from a mixture of not less than 51% corn with malted barley, like a blended Scotch. Some may contain a little rye. The chief distinguishing taste characteristic of bourbon, however, derives from the barrels in which it matures. They are made of American oak, as one would expect; unlike the barrels used for Scotch, however, they are always brand new. Furthermore, they are heavily charred, or toasted, on the insides to a depth of about

WILD TURKEY BOURBON comes from Lawrenceburg, Kentucky

FLAVOURINGS

Discounting the whisky-based liqueurs, the only case of a straight whisky being flavoured is that of certain Canadian products that have minute amounts of other drinks added to them: grape wine, wines from other fruits (prunes are a favourite), unfermented fruit juices, even sherry

MIXING

Old-Fashioned: Grind up a sugar lump with a good shake from the Angostura bottle in the squat tumbler that is named after this drink. Add plenty of ice and a cheering quantity of Canadian or straight rye whisky. Throw in a twist of lemon peel, a slice of orange and a cocktail cherry, and serve with a stirring implement in it.

5mm/¼ in, which allows the spirit freer access to the vanillin and tannins in the wood. Nobody quite knows where the charring tradition came from, but it seems quite likely that it was the result of a happy accident.

There are two distinct styles of bourbon, sweet mash and sour mash, the differences arising at the fermentation stage of the grains. For sweet mash, the yeasts are allowed to perform their work quite quickly over a couple of days, while for sour mash, some yeast from the preceding batch augments the brew. This doubles the length of the fermentation and ensures that more of the sugars in the grain are consumed.

Most bourbon is labelled "Kentucky Straight Bourbon", which means it is made from at least 51% corn, is aged for a minimum of two years in charred new barrels and has been made and matured within the prescribed areas. It is the equivalent category to single malt Scotch. Some, sold as "Blended Straight", is made from more than one lot of straight bourbon, and corresponds to vatted malt. Most bourbon is bottled at a slightly higher strength than standard Scotch – about 43–45% ABV.

The leading brand by a long chalk is Jim Beam, made at Bardstown and virtually synonymous with

bourbon on the export markets. Other brands include Wild Turkey, Evan Williams, Early Times, Old Grand-Dad and the pace-setting Maker's Mark (the one with the top dipped in red sealing-wax).

TENNESSEE

South of the bourbon state of Kentucky, in neighbouring Tennessee, an entirely different but equally distinctive style of whiskey is made. Tennessee sour mash is represented by just two distilleries – Jack Daniel's in Lynchburg, and George Dickel in Tullahoma. Their various bottlings represent some of the richest and smoothest whiskeys made.

Whereas bourbon is matured in charred barrels, Tennessee takes the principle a stage further by actually filtering the newly made spirit through a mass of charcoal. In the yards behind the distilleries, they burn great stacks of sugar maple down to ash and then grind it all into a rough black powder. This is

JACK DANIEL'S
By far the bigger brand of the two Tennessee whiskeys

MAKER'S MARK
Small-volume production allied to top quality

piled to a depth of around 3 metres/10 feet into so-called mellowing vats, all sitting on a fleecy woollen blanket. The whiskey drips at a painfully slow rate from holes in a gridwork of copper pipes above the vats, and filters gradually through the charcoal bed, before being cask-matured in the usual way.

Jack Daniel's is one of the world's best-loved whiskey brands. Its market-leading Old No. 7, in the famous square bottle, first established the kudos of JD by winning a Gold Medal at the 1904 World's Fair in St Louis. Its great rival, Dickel (which spells its product "whisky" in the Scottish way), matures its No. 12 brand for several years longer, and the results are evident in a more discreet and mellower nose and deeper colour. It is bottled at 45% ABV.

One of the great ironies of Tennessee whiskey is that both producers have their distilleries in "dry" counties where it is forbidden to sell alcohol, which means that they may not avail themselves of

JIM BEAM
A particularly
popular bourbon

the doorstep custom they could enjoy from public visits. A glass of soul-saving spring water is offered instead.

IRELAND

The origins of distillation in the Emerald Isle are lost in swathes of Irish mist, but are certainly of great antiquity, at least as old as those of Scotch. There are those who have claimed that it was Irish missionaries who first brought the knowledge of distilling to France, and thus made brandy possible. Whether that is true or not, Irish whiskey once enjoyed an unrivalled reputation as a more approachable style of spirit than Scotch malt. It was only when blended Scotch began to be made on any significant scale towards the end of the 19th century that Irish whiskey was nudged out of the frame.

The reasons for the greater accessibility of Irish whiskey lie in its production process. No peat is used in the kilns, so that there is none of the smoky pungency that is present in some degree in most Scotch. Secondly, punitive taxes on malted barley in the mid-19th century meant that the Irish distillers began to use a mixture of malted and unmalted grain in their mash, making it traditionally a blended product long before the recipes for today's

PADDY
This whiskey is
distilled at
Midleton, just
outside the city
of Cork

CANADIAN CLUB
The leading brand of Canadian whisky.

standard Scotch brands had even been dreamed about.

Most famously of all, Irish whiskey is subjected to a triple distillation by the copper pot still method. The third passage of the spirit through the stills results in a product with a softer, ultra-refined palate profile while still retaining all of its complexity. By law, the whiskey must then be cask-aged for a minimum of three years, although in practice most are aged for two to three times that period. It is usually bottled at 40% ABV.

The brand leader on the export markets is Jameson's. Other notable names include Bushmills, John Power, Murphy's, Paddy, Dunphy's and Tullamore Dew. All but one are made in the Republic, mostly in the environs of Dublin or Cork. The exception is Bushmills, which is located in County Antrim in Northern Ireland.

(There is another Irish "whiskey" of course, made on illegal travelling stills that the authorities have always found notoriously difficult to track down. Perhaps they have more constructive things to do. For all its reputation as toxic brain-scrambler, poteen – pronounced "*pocheen*" – is an unassailable part of Ireland's folk history, and will continue to be so for as long as taxation rates on the official stuff are as rapacious as they are.)

CANADA

Canada's whiskies are made from blends of different grains, the greater proportion of each brand based on an original mash that combines rye, corn and malted barley. They nearly always contain some spirit, however, that is produced entirely from the heavier-tasting rye, but it usually accounts for less than a tenth of the final blend. As a result, they have the reputation of being among the lightest classic whiskies of all, even more so than the triple-distilled Irish.

The whisky industry in Canada dates back only to the last century, when it arose as an offshoot of the agricultural production of grain. It was quite common at one time to pay the millers in kind with some of the grain, and distillation has long been a traditional way of using up surpluses the world over. The earliest

producers – and, despite the country's size, there are still only a handful – were Hiram Walker, Seagram's and Corby's, all in the province of Ontario.

Distillation is by the continuous process, in gigantic column stills. Different spirits produced from different mashes, or fermented from different yeast strains, are painstakingly blended by the distiller – before the maturation in some cases, afterwards in others. All whiskies must spend at least three years in the barrels, which are of new wood, but there is a noble tradition of aged products in Canada for whiskies that are 10, 12, even 18 years old on release. As elsewhere, the standard blends are sold at 40% ABV, but speciality aged bottlings may be somewhat stronger.

A curiosity of Canadian whisky is that the regulations permit the addition of a tiny quantity of other drink products, such as sherry or wine made from grapes or other fruits. While this may account for no more than a hundredth part of the finished product, it makes its presence felt in the fleeting suggestion of fruitiness in the flavours of some whiskies.

CROWN ROYAL
A Canadian brand owned by Seagram's

Most of the distilleries are situated in the eastern provinces of Ontario and Quebec. The leading label is Hiram Walker's Canadian Club, first blended in the 1880s, and is supported by the Burke's and Wiser's ranges from Corby's, McGuinness's Silk Tassel, Alberta Springs and Seagram's Crown Royal.

JAPAN

Of the countries under consideration here, Japan has by far the youngest whisky industry – of even more recent provenance than its efforts at wine making. The first distillery was established only in 1923, and it is only in the last 30 years or so that its products have come to the attention of whisky-drinkers other than the Japanese themselves.

The model for Japan's whiskies is single malt Scotch, but there are equally successful spirits made in the idiom of blended Scotch. The base is a mash of malted barley, dried in kilns fired with a little peat (though considerably less than is the case in Scotland, and so yielding a less aromatically defined product). Distillation is by the pot still method. Some of the brands are aged in used sherry or bourbon casks, as for Scotch, others in heavily charred new American oak barrels, as for bourbon itself. Some distilleries buy in a proportion of unused Scottish spirit for blending in with the home-grown whisky. The premium brands

SUNTORY
The 12-year-old
Yamazaki is a
kind of Japanese
single malt

are generally bottled at around 43% ABV.

The giant drinks company Suntory, which has a finger in all sorts of pies from classed-growth Bordeaux to the green melon liqueur Midori, is also the biggest producer of Japanese whisky, accounting for virtually three-quarters of the industry's annual output. Behind Suntory comes the Nikka company, and then the smaller producers Sanraku Ocean and Seagram's, which is anything but small everywhere else.

In Japan, whisky is nearly always taken heavily watered. Whereas in Scotland, the mix is usually half-and-half, the Japanese prefer to take it as a long pale-yellowish drink in tall glasses filled to the top with spring water and with plenty of ice – about the most denatured form in which fine whisky is commonly drunk anywhere in the world. It is drunk both as an aperitif and as an accompaniment to food.

Among the more illustrious products are Suntory's 12-year-old Pure Malt from its Yamazaki distillery on Honshu, the principal island; Nikka Memorial 50, Sanraku Ocean's single malt Karuizawa (also from Honshu); and Seagram's top labels Crescent and Emblem.

LIQUEURS

SINCE WE ARE CLEARLY distinguishing between spirits and liqueurs, it would be useful to arrive at a working definition of what constitutes a liqueur. Why is Kirsch a spirit, for example, but cherry brandy a liqueur?

The distinction lies in the way that the various flavours of these drinks are obtained. Essentially, a liqueur is any spirit-based drink to which flavouring elements have been added, usually by infusion, and – in the vast majority of cases – enhanced by sweetening. Sometimes the flavourings are themselves subjected to distillation; sometimes they are merely soaked or macerated in an alcohol base. Although there are

flavoured spirits, such as lemon vodka (or, for that matter, gin) there are no *un*flavoured liqueurs. To answer the question in the first paragraph, Kirsch is a spirit because it is a straight, unsweetened distillate of cherries, whereas cherry brandy is a neutral spirit from other sources to which cherry flavour is added by infusion of the fruit.

Liqueurs have their origins in the practice of adding aromatic ingredients – herbs, fruit extracts, seeds, spices, nuts, roots, flowers, and so forth – to the earliest distilled spirits, in order both to mask the unappealing flavour of the impurities that had not been rectified out of them, and to endow the resulting

potions with medicinal value. Given a source of basic spirit, they could and often would be concocted in domestic kitchens for use in cooking as well as for drinking – a tradition carried on in this book. As various proprietary liqueurs came on to the market during the course of the 19th century, so home liqueur-making declined.

When the science of distillation was still in its infancy in Europe, the Catalan physician Arnaldo de Vilanova advanced the theory that steeping them in alcohol extracted the beneficial qualities of certain medicinal herbs. This was a logical progression of the non-alcoholic distilling of essential oils that had been practised in ancient Egypt and classical Greece. As an offshoot of the alchemical arts, distilling was intimately bound up with the doomed enterprise of attempting to turn base metals to gold, and so gold itself came to play a part in the formulation of alcohol-based remedies. (Arnaldo was saved from the Inquisition, it is said, because he had cured the Pope of life-threatening illness by means of a tonic containing flakes of

Left: Le Palais de Bénédictine. Until recently Bénédictine was still made by the monastic order. Chartreuse is one of the few liqueurs still produced in the traditional way in the distillery (below) at Voiron, near Grenoble.

Above: Even today, small producers, such as this French artisan distiller, produce a wonderful variety of flavoured liqueurs.

gold.) The tradition lives on today in the form of a drink called Goldwasser.

It was in the religious orders that many of the traditional liqueurs were first formulated, since the medicinal ingredients used were often grown in the monastery gardens. By the late Middle Ages, the Italians had become the most celebrated practitioners of the art of liqueur-making. The marriage of Catherine de Medici to the future French king Henri II in 1533, brought a wave of Italians into France, bringing their expertise with them. Some of the more notable products, such as Bénédictine, were made by French monastic orders until relatively recently. (Chartreuse still is.)

In the last century, liqueurs had an aura of being soothingly palatable after-dinner digestifs for those – women essentially – who were not fond of the stronger alternatives such as cognac.

Indeed, they were seen as more ladylike drinks altogether, an image enhanced by the introduction of the tiny glasses that are still depressingly enough seen as the appropriate receptacles. By now, they had shed most of their health-giving claims and become honest-to-goodness drinks, although it was still popularly believed by imbibers that they had prophylactic properties.

The cocktail era of the 1920s and 30s that had doggedly to contend with universal prohibition in the USA, but suffered no such constraints in London, Paris, Berlin and Venice, freed liqueurs from the straitjacket of cultured politeness in which the Victorian period had imprisoned them. At a stroke, they transformed the old slings and fizzes, fixes, sours, punches, cups and smashes into drinks that were worthy of their names. A mixture of gin with lemon juice, sugar

Above: The museum of La Grande Chartreuse Monastery, Isère, France.

and soda may have been a pleasant way of taking gin, but add a slug of cherry brandy to it and it became an altogether more exciting and hazardous proposition. That sense of playing with fire is inscribed in the names of the great cocktail recipes of the 1920s, in their evocations of gambling (Casino), sex (Maiden's Blush), spiritual danger (Hell, Little Devil) and even First World War munitions (Whizzbang, Depth Bomb, Artillery).

No drinking culture was ever happier or more heedless than that of the original and greatest cocktail era, and it couldn't have happened without the liqueurs. The following pages are a taster's tour of the famous and the not so famous.

ADVOCAAT

ADVOCAAT IS A Dutch speciality. It is essentially a customized version of the humble egg nog, without the milk: a mixture of simple grape brandy with egg yolks and sugar, as thick and as yellow as tinned custard. Most of it is sold in this natural form, although it is possible in the Netherlands to buy vanilla- and fruit-flavoured versions. As a result of its velvety texture and bland wholesomeness, advocaat is often thought of as a drink for the elderly, and is commonly added to mugs of hot chocolate or strong coffee.

There are a few widely available brands of advocaat on the market: the red-labelled Warninks is probably the most familiar, but Fockinks, and the liqueur specialists, Bols and De Kuypers, also make it. The standard bottled strength is quite low for a liqueur – around 17% ABV, which is about the same strength as the average fortified wine.

*WARNINKS
Probably the
most famous
advocaat brand*

HOW TO SERVE
In the Netherlands, advocaat is drunk both as aperitif and digestif. Unmixed, its texture is such that it is often consumed with a teaspoon. Taken in a hot beverage, it makes a comforting bedtime drink.

MIXING
Snowball: Put a generous measure (a couple of fluid ounces) of advocaat in a tall glass and top up with ice-cold sparkling lemonade. If you require a bit more of a kick, add a dessertspoon of sweet brown sherry to it as well. (This is the kind of "cocktail" generally considered safe to give to minors, since it resembles nothing so much as a particularly rich milkshake.)

HOW IT IS MADE
Commercial grape spirit is bought in and sweetened with sugar syrup. Only the yolks of the eggs are added, along with an emulsifying agent to prevent the mixture from separating.

TASTES GOOD WITH
As the ready-made basis of an egg nog, it can be made into a long drink by topping it up with whole milk and a sprinkling of nutmeg.

ADVOCAAT
This is the only manufactured drink in this book to contain egg yolk.

AMARETTO

OF ALL THE LIQUEURS that rely on almonds for their principal flavouring, amaretto is the most famous. It has become widely associated in people's minds with one particular Italian brand, Disaronno Amaretto, made by a company called Illva, although there are other liqueurs that may properly be called amarettos. The famous amaretto comes in a rectangular bottle, with a label in the form of an old scroll and a disproportionately large, square screwtop. The flavour is not entirely derived from almonds but from the stones of apricots too. Resembling a kind of liquid marzipan, the taste is strong and sweet and is quite assertive even when mixed in a cocktail.

Legend has it that the recipe was given to an Italian painter, Bernardino Luini, in the 16th century by an innkeeper who was the model for the Virgin Mary in his wall-painting of the Nativity at Saronno. Whether or not there is much truth in the tale, the original domestic concoction was probably grape brandy in which apricot kernels – with their strongly almondy flavour – had been steeped.

HOW IT IS MADE

Almond extracts, along with apricot kernels and seeds, are steeped in brandy, and the resulting drink is sweetened with sugar syrup and coloured to a deep brown.

DISARONNO AMARETTO
The most famous brand of Italian amaretto

MIXING

Godmother: Mix Disaronno Amaretto with an equal measure of vodka in a tumbler full of ice.
Godfather (below): As above, but substitute Scotch for the vodka.

TASTES GOOD WITH

Just as a frangipane mixture, full of ground almonds, makes a good base for almost any fruit tart, so amaretto works well in the syrup for a fruit salad, or added to whipped cream or ice cream for most fruit-based desserts. It also marries deliciously with chocolate in super-rich *pot au chocolat*, and is excellent in a liqueur coffee, and perhaps with cognac too.

CASONI AMARETTO
Amaretto's flavour is like marzipan in a bottle

OTHER NAMES
France: crème d'amandes

FLAVOURINGS
Almonds
Apricots

HOW TO SERVE
Although sweet, the flavour of Disaronno Amaretto is quite complex enough for it to be enjoyable on its own, but it works better chilled. Serving it *frappé* (poured over crushed ice) is highly refreshing.

ANIS

FLAVOURINGS
Anise berries (aniseed).
Sometimes the seeds of
star anise – an oriental
shrub that bears a fruit
in the shape of an
eight-pointed star –
may be used. The
flavour is fairly similar,
though by no means
identical

CONFUSION REIGNS as to the precise differences between anis and pastis, and indeed whether there are any meaningful differences at all. They are both flavoured with the berries of the aniseed plant, originally native to North Africa, and are popular all around the Mediterranean. They both turn cloudy when watered, and are both claimed as the respectable successor to the outlawed absinthe.

One august authority claims that pastis should be flavoured with liquorice rather than aniseed, although the two are very close in taste. Another claims that anis is simply one of the types of pastis. Still another claims that, whereas anis is a product of the maceration of aniseed or liquorice in spirit, pastis should properly be seen as a distillation from either of the two ingredients themselves.

They can't all be right of course, but for what it's worth, I incline to accept the last definition. For one thing, anis tends to be lower in alcohol than pastis – liqueur strength rather than spirit strength. The one thing we can be sure of

HOW TO SERVE
The only true way to
serve anis is to take it
ice-cold in a little thick-
bottomed tumbler. The
addition of a small
amount of water –
usually about as much
again – turns it milky
but with a faint green-
ish tinge. It is
considered a great
appetite-whetter.

OTHER NAMES
France: Anise *Spain*: Anís

is that pastis is always French (the word is old southern French dialect), whereas anis – particularly with that spelling – can also be Spanish. In Spain, there are sweet and dry varieties, whereas French anise tends mainly to be dry.

Ever since the days of the medical school of Salerno, and probably earlier, extract of anis has been seen as a valuable weapon in the apothecary's armoury. It is thought to be especially good for ailments of the stomach.

ANISETTE
Anisette is quite definitely a liqueur. It is French, sweetened, and usually somewhat stronger than anis. The most famous brand is Marie Brizard, from the firm named after the Bordelaise who, in the mid-18th century, was given the recipe by a West Indian acquaintance.

ANIS
*This liqueur is
made in Spain
as well as
France*

ANISETTE
*The sweet
liqueur form of
anis, typified by
this Marie
Brizard anisette*

AURUM

IF THE NAME of Argentarium evokes silver, that of Aurum hints at gold. One glance at its colour will explain why. Made in the Abruzzi mountains, on the Adriatic coast of Italy, Aurum is a brandy-based proprietary liqueur in which a mixture of orange peel and whole oranges is infused, and the lustrous golden intensity of its appearance enhanced by saffron. It is claimed that the basic formula is of great antiquity. Aurum was given its Latin name by the celebrated Italian writer Gabriele d'Annunzio. The name hints that it may at one time have contained particles of genuine gold, harking back to the alchemical origins of distillation, and it has logically been argued that Aurum was the true forerunner of Goldwasser.

HOW IT IS MADE

No mere industrial spirit is used in Aurum. The brandy in it is distilled by the makers from vintage Italian wines, and the distillate is cask-aged for around four years to take up wood colour. The oranges (and other citrus fruits) are infused separately in more brandy, and then the infusion is triple-distilled. This, and the first brandy, are then blended and allowed another period of oak maturation.

ARGENTARIUM
One of a handful of liqueurs that are still produced by religious orders, Argentarium is made in a monastery in the Lazio region of Italy, north of Rome. It is based on grape brandy, flavoured with a collection of herbs that grow wild on the surrounding hillsides, some of which are gathered by the monks themselves. Most of it is consumed locally.

BENEDICTINE

"*DEO OPTIMO MAXIMO*" (Praise be to God, most good, most great), exclaimed the Benedictine monk, who formulated the liqueur that now bears his order's name, on first tasting the results. Or so the story goes. It was reputedly in 1510, so it isn't easy to verify. What is certain is that his monastery at Fécamp, in the Normandy region of northern France, produced this cognac-based herbal liqueur until the time of the French Revolution in 1789, when the monasteries were forcibly closed and production banned.

Bénédictine was officially extinct until the 1860s, when it was revived by a descendent of the monastery's lawyers, Alexandre Le Grand. On finding the secret recipe among a bundle of yellowing papers, he was inspired to build an extraordinary new distillery in the high Gothic style at Fécamp, and the now secularized liqueur – first christened Bénédictine by Le Grand – lived to fight another day.

Bénédictine is a bright golden potion of honeyed sweetness, containing a herbalist's pantheon of medicinal plants and spices. The exact formula is known only to three people at any given time, but it is thought to contain as many as 75 aromatizing ingredients.

GOLDEN AURUM comes from Abruzzo, eastern Italy

HOW TO SERVE
It is imperative to serve a speciality product such as **Aurum** (below) by itself as a digestif. It should not be chilled but rather warmed in the hand like fine cognac, and served in the same sort of glass to appreciate its aromas.

Bénédictine should ideally be served straight in a large liqueur glass at the end of a meal, but its makers clearly have no qualms about its use as a mixing ingredient by those who find the sweetness of classic liqueurs too much to take *au naturel*.

BENEDICTINE One of the old monastic liqueurs

CHARTREUSE

Unlike BENEDICTINE, CHARTREUSE really is still made by monks – of the Carthusian order – at Voiron, near Grenoble, not far from the site of their monastery, La Grande Chartreuse. Expelled from France at the time of the French Revolution, the order was allowed back into the mother country after the defeat of Napoleon, only to be kicked out again in 1903. It was then that a second branch of the operation was founded at Tarragona, in eastern Spain, and it continued as Chartreuse's second address until 1991, long after the production was finally re-established in France in 1932.

The Carthusians are a silent order, which has no doubt helped to keep the recipe a secret; like its Norman counterpart, it is known only to a lucky trio. Proceeds from the worldwide sales of Chartreuse are ploughed back into the order's funds, from where it goes to pay for all kinds of charitable works.

There is a premium version of Chartreuse (the original recipe is said to date from 1605) called Elixir, which is sold in miniature bottles at a fearsome 71% ABV, but it is principally sold in two incarnations today, green (55%) and yellow (40%). The latter is a deep greenish-yellow hue, sweet, honeyed and slightly minty in flavour; while the green Chartreuse is a pale, leafy colour, has a less pungent herbal scent and is distinctly less viscous.

Additionally, the order produces a rare higher grade of each colour, labelled VEP, for *vieillissement exceptionnellement prolongé* (exceptionally long ageing).

GREEN CHARTREUSE
Intensely powerful and aromatic.

YELLOW CHARTREUSE
Sweeter than green Chartreuse and of normal spirit strength.

MIXING
Alaska: Shake three-quarters gin to one-quarter yellow Chartreuse with ice and strain into a cocktail glass.

Bijou: Stir equal measures of Plymouth gin, green Chartreuse and sweet red vermouth with ice and a dash of orange bitters in a mixing jug. Strain into a cocktail glass. Add a cherry and a twist of lemon.

HOW IT IS MADE

By varying processes of distillation, infusion and maceration, over 130 herbs and plants are used to flavour a base of grape brandy. They were all once gathered from the mountains surrounding the monastery, but some are now imported from Italy and Switzerland. It is aged in casks for up to five years, except for the VEP, which receives twice that long.

TASTES GOOD WITH

The French sometimes fortify their hot chocolate with a reviving splash of the green Chartreuse. The yellow is thought more suitable for coffee.

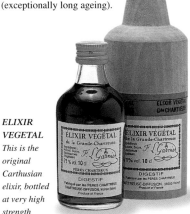

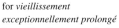

HOW TO SERVE
If you find Chartreuse overwhelming on its own, do as the French do and serve it mixed as a long drink with tonic or soda and plenty of ice.

ELIXIR VEGETAL
This is the original Carthusian elixir, bottled at very high strength

COINTREAU

ONE OF THE MOST POPULAR branded liqueurs of all, Cointreau is, properly speaking, a variety of Curaçao. This means it is a brandy-based spirit that has been flavoured with the peel of bitter oranges. When it was launched in 1849 by the Cointreau brothers, Edouard and Adolphe, it was sold under the brand name Triple Sec White Curaçao, but so many other proprietary Curaçaos began to be sold as Triple Sec that the family decided to give it their own name instead.

The centre of operations, as well as a distillery, are located in Angers, in the Loire valley, but it is also made in the Americas. A variety of different bottlings is made at different strengths, including a cream version, but the best-loved Cointreau is the one that comes in a square dark-brown bottle at 40% ABV.

COINTREAU
One of the best-loved liqueurs of them all

MIXING
Cointreau is so versatile in cocktails that a list of recipes could easily fill a whole book. Suffice to say it can successfully be mixed in equal quantities with virtually any spirit (except perhaps whisky) and the juice of half a lemon and shaken with ice. Start with gin and you have a **White Lady** (below), brandy for a **Sidecar**, vodka for a **Balalaika** and even tequila for a lemon (as opposed to lime) **Margarita**.

Despite its spirit strength, Cointreau tastes deliciously innocuous. It is sugar-sweet and colourless, but has a powerful fume of fresh oranges, with an underlying vaguely herbal note too. The oranges used in it are a clever blend of bitter green Seville-style varieties from the Caribbean (the island of Curaçao itself is close to Venezuela) and sweeter types from the south of France.

HOW IT IS MADE
Cointreau is a double distillation of grape brandy, infused with orange peel, sweetened and further aromatized with other secret plant ingredients.

TASTES GOOD WITH
If the balance of other seasonings is right, it works admirably in the orange sauce classically served with duck. It is excellent in a range of desserts, particularly so in rich chocolate mousse.

HOW TO SERVE
Absolutely everybody's favourite way of serving Cointreau is either on the rocks or *frappé*, depending on whether you like your ice in chunks or crystals. The cold then mitigates some of the sweetness of the liqueur, while the pure citrus flavour is exquisitely refreshing.

CREAM LIQUEURS

CREAM LIQUEURS ARE an ever-expanding category in the contemporary market. Whether the makers acknowledge it or not, cream liqueurs all owe something of their inspiration and appeal to the archetypal brand, Bailey's Irish Cream. The manufacturers tend to push them particularly at Christmas, where they occupy a niche as the soft option for those who feel they need a spoonful of sugar and a dollop of cream to help the alcohol go down.

Bailey's itself is a blend of Irish whiskey and cream flavoured with coffee. It became suddenly chic in the 1970s, but was quickly saddled with the image of the kind of soft, svelte drink that unscrupulous boys plied unsuspecting girls with in nightclubs. Since then, cream liqueurs have gone on multiplying.

Coffee and chocolate flavourings are particularly common, and indeed some cream liqueurs are made by confectionery companies, such as Cadbury's and Terry's. Then again, some of the more reputable liqueur-makers have produced cream versions of their own top products (for example, Crème de Grand Marnier) in order to grab a share of this evidently lucrative market.

I have to say I decline to take these products seriously. At best, they are substitutes for real cream cocktails, but they are always sweeter and less powerful than the genuine home-made article, and many of them contain an artificial stabilizer to stop the cream from separating. In any case, why rely on somebody else's formula when you can follow your own specifications? Once you have made your own brandy Alexanders, you won't want chocolate cream liqueur.

The extreme was reached when another Irish drinks company of some repute launched a product called Sheridan's in the early 1990s. It came in a bifurcated bottle with two tops, one half filled with a black liquid that was coffee-flavoured Irish whiskey, the other with thick white cream. The idea was that you poured first from one side of the bottle and then from the other – remembering to screw the top back on to the first half – in order to simulate the appearance of a liqueur coffee. (Little matter that Irish coffee is supposed to be served hot.) I am told the product has not so far proved conspicuously successful, perhaps because it involves such a fandango when it comes to serving it in bars.

BAILEY'S
The daddy
of all cream
liqueurs

CADBURY'S
CREAM
LIQUEUR
A ready-made
brandy
Alexander at
a pinch

CREME LIQUEURS

A WHOLE RANGE OF liqueurs that use the prefix *"crème de"* may be bracketed together here. They are nothing at all to do with cream liqueurs, despite the terminology. They nearly always consist of one dominant flavour indicated in the name, often but not always a fruit, and are usually appropriately coloured. In the main, they are bottled at 25–30% ABV, and may be considered among the more useful building-blocks of the cocktail-mixer's repertoire.

Originally, the term "crème" was used to indicate that these were sweetened liqueurs, as distinct from dry spirits such as cognac or calvados. They were mainly French in origin – the Marie Brizard

FRAISE DES BOIS
This version of crème de fraise uses wild strawberries

MIXING
The use of these liqueurs in cocktail-making is as limitless as the flavours themselves. Sometimes they work well with each other (try brown cacao and fraise, or banane and noyau, for example) but they will need a very dry base to counteract the cumulative impact of the sweetness. They all work well in cream cocktails, but one flavour is usually quite sufficient. Let your imagination off the leash.

Fruit Daiquiri: The original Daiquiri recipe of white rum shaken with the juice of half a lemon and a pinch of sugar can be adapted by adding a measure of any of the fruit liqueurs to it (and perhaps some puréed fruit as well), but you may then want to leave out the sugar.

Stinger: The adaptable Stinger is simply a half-and-half mixture of any spirit with white crème de menthe, shaken with ice and served over smashed ice in a cocktail glass. The prototype version is probably with cognac.

Alexander: The recipe for this given in the brandy chapter can be adapted with other spirits too – gin is particularly successful – but it is always the brown crème de cacao that must be used.

FLAVOURINGS
The flavours of such liqueurs are numerous, and the following list does not pretend to be exhaustive. The French names are given first, since that is how they are labelled.
Most commonly seen are: crème de banane (banana), cacao (cocoa or chocolate – comes in dark brown and white versions), cassis (blackcurrant), fraise (strawberry), framboise (raspberry) and menthe (mint – comes in bright green and white versions).

company founded in the mid-18th century in Bordeaux is still important in this field – but production soon spread to other specialist liqueur manufacturers such as Bols and De Kuypers of Holland.

Before the widespread availability of such products, the sweetening element in a cocktail used to be sugar, pure and simple, or perhaps a sugar syrup. The crème liqueurs had the advantage of not only providing that sweetness, but also of introducing another flavour into the drinks they were added to. They have since become indispensable in extending the horizons of both the professional and amateur bartender, and are usually a recommended purchase in any guide giving advice on starting your own cocktail bar at home.

Most of these products will be based on a neutral-tasting, un-aged grape brandy, with the various flavouring ingredients either infused or

CRÈME DE FRAISE

A basic strawberry liqueur from Marie Brizard of Bordeaux.

HOW TO SERVE

If these drinks are to be taken as befitted their original purpose, as pleasant aids to digestion at the end of a grand dinner, they are best served *frappé* – i.e. poured over shaved ice – rather than neat. In that way, some of their sugary sweetness is mitigated.

MIXING

Oracabessa: Shake a measure of dark rum with a measure of crème de banane and the juice of half a lemon with ice and strain into a tall glass. Float some thin slices of banana on the surface of the drink and top it up with sparkling lemonade. Garnish lavishly with fruits.

Silver Jubilee: Shake equal measures of gin, crème de banane and cream with ice and strain into a cocktail glass.

Blackout (from Lucius Beebe's *Stork Club Bar Book*): Shake a measure and three-quarters of gin and three-quarters of a measure of crème de mûre with the juice of half a lime and plenty of ice and strain into a cocktail glass.

Stratosphere: A few dashes of crème de violette are added to a glass of champagne until a mauve colour is obtained. The scent-edness is then enhanced by adding a whole clove to the glass. (An American violet liqueur, Crème Yvette, was at one time the only correct product to use in this very ladylike aperitif.)

English Rose: Shake a measure and a half of London gin with three-quarters of a measure of crème de roses, the juice of half a lemon, half a teaspoon of caster sugar and half an egg-white, with ice, and strain into a wine glass. (Alternatively, you can make this in an electric blender for that extra frothiness.)

CRÈME DE CACAO

Cacao – cocoa or chocolate – is available in two versions, dark and white, to please the chocoholics.

macerated in the spirit rather than being subject to distillation themselves. The difference, essentially, between infusion and maceration is that the former involves some gentle heating action, while the latter is just a cold soaking of the flavouring element in the spirit until it has been broken down and has imparted its aromatic compounds. Maceration is obviously a considerably slower process than infusion. In both cases, the ingre-dient has to be rendered water-soluble, in the case of maceration particularly so.

Since these are intended to be rich but simple products, with one overriding flavour, the crème liqueurs are not generally treated to

CREME DE BANANE
Banana is one of the more versatile flavours

ageing in wood. Oak maturation would inter-fere anyway with the often bold primary colours of the drinks, as well as obscuring the tastes.

They are more often than not sold in 50cl bottles. You will find as you use them that a certain amount of powdery sugar deposit builds up underneath the screw tops; simply give them a good wipe down every now and then.

HOW THEY ARE MADE

After the infusion or maceration, during which take-up of flavour is obtained, the aromatized spirit may then have to be strained to remove any solid particles caused by making the

CREME DE CASSIS
Cassis is also a speciality of Burgundy

MIXING

Kir: The world-famous aperitif created in Burgundy, and originally named after a mayor of Dijon, consists of a glass of light, dry, acidic white wine with a teaspoon or two (depending on taste) of crème de cassis. The classic wine to use is a Bourgogne Aligoté of the most recent vintage, but any fairly neutral-tasting but *sharp* white wine will do. Add the cassis to a glass of non-vintage Brut champagne and the drink becomes a **Kir Royale** (below).

CRÈME DE FRAMBOISE

Red fruit liqueurs, such as framboise, are very good if added by the teaspoon to a glass of basic champagne or sparkling wine.

FLAVOURINGS

More obscure flavours include: crème d'ananas (pineapple), café (coffee), mandarine (tangerine), mûre (blackberry), myrtille (bilberry), noyau (almond), roses (rose-petal), thé (tea), vanille (vanilla), violette (violet)

flavouring agent water-soluble. It is then sweetened, usually by means of the addition of sugar solution, or sometimes with a sugar and glucose mix. Unless it is possible to achieve a striking colour naturally (which is in fact quite rare), the colour is then created by the addition of vegetable-based colouring matter such as carotene or beetroot. Red colourings are often created by adding cochineal. These colourings do not affect the flavour. The liqueur is then subjected to a heavy filtration to ensure a bright, crystal-clear product. It is transferred into neutral, stainless steel tanks to await bottling.

CREME DE MURE
A richly flavoured blackberry liqueur.

CREME DE MENTHE
Green crème de menthe is sweet and spearminty

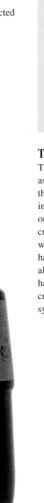

CREME DE PECHE
Peach is an unusual flavour to find in a crème liqueur.

MIXING
Grasshopper: Shake equal measures of green crème de menthe, white crème de cacao and thick cream with ice and strain into a cocktail glass.

TASTES GOOD WITH
The most obvious way to use these liqueurs is as boosting ingredients in desserts that are themselves flavoured with the same principal ingredient, especially in the case of the fruit ones. Enliven your strawberry mousse with crème de fraise, your blackberry cheesecake with crème de mûre, and so forth. (On the other hand, a richly gooey *pot au chocolat* can get along quite well without crème de cacao if you have used top-quality chocolate.) The flowery crème liqueurs make exotic additions to the syrup for a simple fruit salad.

BRAMBLE
Fruit liqueurs are also made in the UK.

CURACAO

FIRST INVENTED BY THE DUTCH, Curaçao was a white rum-based liqueur flavoured with the peel of bitter green oranges found by the settlers on the Caribbean island of the same name, not far off the coast of Venezuela. Despite its geographically specific name, the liqueur has never been subject to anything like appellation regulations. It is made by many different companies in a number of countries, where brandy is used as the starter spirit.

A variant name in common use was Triple Sec,

ORANGE
CURACAO
All Curaçao is
flavoured with
bitter oranges

MIXING

Olympic: Shake equal measures of cognac, orange Curaçao and freshly squeezed orange juice with ice and strain into a cocktail glass. Decorate with a twist of orange peel.
Oasis: Pour a double measure of gin over ice-cubes in a tall glass. Add half a measure of blue Curaçao. Top up with tonic water and stir well. Garnish with a slice of lemon and sprig of mint.

FLAVOURING

the most famous example being Cointreau, although confusingly Curaçao is not at all *sec* but always sweet. The bitterness of the oranges – which are green simply because they are not quite ripe, not because they are some notably exotic variety – balances the sweetness, however, to the extent that drinkers may have been prepared to consider it dry.

Curaçao comes in a range of colours in addition to the clear version. The orange Curaçao, especially from companies like Bols, is often particularly bitter, its colour a deep, burnished tawny orange. Curaçao also comes in bright blue, dark green, red and yellow versions for novelty value, but the flavour is always of orange. The strength is generally somewhere between 25–30% ABV.

The name of the island is not, of course, Dutch but Portuguese, after the original discoverers. More perplexity is occasioned over the correct way to pronounce "Curaçao" than over the name of any other liqueur. It should properly be "curashow" (to rhyme with "miaow"), but it is corrupted by English speakers into something like "cura-say-oh".

HOW TO SERVE

The bitterness of the fruit mixes well with other bitter flavours, so orange Curaçao and tonic makes a particularly appetizing long drink. Alternatively, use a not-too-sweet sparkling lemonade, if you can find one. It also goes well in equal measures with either dry or sweet vermouth. Curaçao is not especially pleasant taken neat.

Triple Sec (only for the colourless version,
strictly speaking)

HOW IT IS MADE
The blossom and dried peel of wild oranges are
steeped in grape brandy or even neutral spirit;
the resulting infusion is then sweetened,
clarified and
coloured accord-
ing to style.

CURACAO
Blue Curaçao enjoyed
something of a vogue
in the cocktail renais-
sance of the early
1980s, though its
colour makes it hard to
mix with.

TRIPLE SEC
The term tends
to be used for
the colourless
Curaçao

MIXING
Whip: Shake equal measures of cognac, dry
vermouth and white Curaçao with a dash of
pastis (e.g. Pernod) and plenty of ice and
strain into a cocktail glass. (It should be noted
that this lethal cocktail contains no non-alcoholic ingredient. Caution is advised.)
Rite of Spring (below): Mix a double
measure of vodka and a measure of green
Curaçao with ice in a mixing-jug. Decant into
a tall glass and top up with clear lemonade.
Dangle a long twist of lemon peel in the drink.

TASTES GOOD WITH
Indispensable in the classic crêpe Suzette. In the
recipe given by the great French chef Auguste
Escoffier, the pancake batter is flavoured with
tangerine juice and Curaçao and the cooked
crêpe sauced with butter, sugar and tangerine
zests. These days, it is generally Cointreau that is
used in this ever-popular dessert.

CUARANTA Y TRES
Cuaranta is a sweet liqueur made in the
Cartagena region of eastern Spain, based on a
recipe that supposedly dates from classical
times when the Phoenicians founded
Carthage, in North Africa, and introduced
viticulture. It is concocted from a brandy
base with infusions of herbs, but has a noticeably predominant flavour of vanilla, which
rather torpedoes the Carthaginian theory
since vanilla was only discovered in the 16th
century by Spanish explorers in Mexico. Not
much seen outside its region of production, it
is nonetheless held in high regard locally.

DRAMBUIE

Drambuie is Scotland's (and, for that matter, Britain's) pre-eminent contribution to the world's classic liqueurs. Hugely popular in the United States, it is a unique and inimitable concoction of Scotch whisky, heather honey and herbs. The story goes that the recipe was given as a reward to one Captain Mackinnon in 1745, after the defeat at Culloden by Charles Edward Stuart – or Bonnie Prince Charlie, as the pretender to the English throne has ever since been better known. The lad that was born to be king was of course ferried to Skye, and from thence to France, away from the clutches of the nefarious English. Captain Mackinnon was his protector.

That story has inevitably since been debunked by meticulous historians. The truth is almost certainly the other way round. It was the Mackinnons who revived the spirits of the fugitive Prince with their own Scotch-based home concoction, which was very much a typical blend of the period, an unrefined spirit disguised with sweet and herbal additives.

Today, the spirit is anything but unrefined, being a mixture of fine malt and straight grain whiskies, to which the flavourings are added. The Mackinnon family still makes it, though near Edinburgh now rather than on Skye. They registered its name (from the Gaelic *an dram buidheach*, "the drink that satisfies") in 1892. It has been in private production since the time of the Bonnie Prince, but was only launched commercially in 1906 – with spectacular success.

TASTES GOOD WITH
A hunk of rich Dundee cake doused in Drambuie is a sumptuous cold-weather treat.

DRAMBUIE
Perhaps
Britain's
greatest
contribution to
the liqueur
world

CYNAR
Cynar is a liqueur for the very brave. It is a soupy, dark-brown potion made in Italy, which is flavoured with artichoke hearts (its name derives from the Latin for artichoke, *cynarum*). All of the savoury bitterness of the globe artichoke, boldly illustrated on its label, is in it, and if that sounds like fun, go ahead and try it. I once swallowed a modest measure of it in a little backstreet bar in Venice, and of all my shimmering memories of the watery city, Cynar is not, I have to say, the loveliest.

HOW TO SERVE
Serve Drambuie as it comes, over ice, or with an equal measure of Scotch as a **Rusty Nail**.

GALLIANO

ANOTHER OF ITALY'S liqueur specialities, golden-yellow Galliano is chiefly known on the international cocktail scene for its matchless role of livening up a vodka-and-orange in the Harvey Wallbanger cocktail, and for its tall conical bottle. It was invented by one Arturo Vaccari, a Tuscan distiller who named his new creation in honour of an Italian soldier, Major Giuseppe Galliano. In 1895 Galliano held out under siege at Enda Jesus in Ethiopia for 44 days against the vastly superior Abyssinian forces under the command of Haile Selassie's nephew.

The formula, as we are accustomed to hear in the world of liqueurs, is a jealously guarded secret, but it is said to be based on up to 80 herbs, roots,

GALLIANO
This Italian classic comes in a distinctive conical bottle

berries and flowers from the alpine slopes to the north of Italy. Among its flavours is a strong presence of anise or liquorice, and there is a pronounced scent of vanilla. It is also naturally very sweet. Despite the complexity of its tastes, it is a valuable addition to the bartender's battery.

HOW IT IS MADE

The various flavouring ingredients are steeped in a mixture of neutral spirit and water and then distilled; the resulting potion is then blended with refined spirits. It is bottled at 35% ABV.

FIOR D'ALPI

No liqueur makes more of a show of itself than Fior d'Alpi. Made in northern Italy, its name means "Alpine flowers", and those – along with a fistful of wild herbs – are its principal flavourings. It is a delicate primrose hue and comes in a tall narrow bottle. What catches the eye in the shop window, though, is the gnarled little tree that sits inside every bottle. If you leave the bottle undisturbed for a while, the sugar in the drink will form a crystallized frosting on the twigs that can look touchingly Christmassy. That, coupled with the agreeable sweetness of the liqueur itself, is what keeps it popular – at least in Italy. Similar products are sold as Millefiori and – what else? – Edelweiss.

GLAYVA

LIKE DRAMBUIE, Glayva is a Scotch whisky-based liqueur made near Edinburgh, but it is of much more recent provenance. The drink was first formulated just after the Second World War. Its aromatizers are quite similar to those of Drambuie, although its flavour is intriguingly different. Heather honey and various herbs are used, and so is a quantity of orange peel, resulting in a noticeably fruitier attack on the palate.

The noble Scot commemorated in the case of Glayva is one Master Borthwick, the phlegmatic 16-year-old credited with carrying Robert the Bruce's heart back to Scotland after the King's defeat at the hands of the Saracens. Not content

MIXING

Saracen: Shake a measure of Scotch whisky, half a measure each of Glayva and dry sherry and a dash of orange bitters with ice. Pour into a tumbler and add a splash of soda. Decorate with a piece of orange rind.

with rescuing the regal heart, the indomitable lad cut off the head of a Saracen chieftain he had killed, impaled it on a spear, and brought that back too just to keep his spirits up. All of those pubs named the Saracen's Head recall the event, as did the Moorish head once depicted on the Glayva label.

TASTES GOOD WITH

Like the other Scotch-based liqueurs, Glayva is particularly good added to an ice cream, perhaps one flavoured with honey and/or orange, like the drink itself.

FLAVOURINGS
Heather honey
Orange peel
Various herbs

HOW TO SERVE
Glayva should be served just as it is, in a standard whisky tumbler. Its fruitiness makes it slightly better for chilling than Drambuie, but don't overdo it.

GLAYVA
The original formula for
Glayva is much older than
the product itself

GOLDWASSER

GOLDWASSER, OR Danziger Goldwasser to give it its archetypal name, recalls the great Catalan physician Arnaldo de Villanova who, in the 13th century, is reputed to have cured the Pope of a dangerous illness by giving him a herbal elixir containing specks of gold. In so doing, he also saved his own skin from the Inquisition. Since the search for the elixir of life was intimately bound up with alchemy's project of turning base metals into gold, it was only natural that gold itself should be seen as being beneficial to health.

FLAVOURINGS
Aniseed
Caraway seeds
Citrus fruits

GOLDWASSER
All Goldwasser came
originally from Gdansk,
like this one

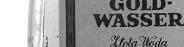

OTHER NAMES
France: Liqueur d'Or or eau d'or

MIXING
Generally, there is no point in mixing Goldwasser because you then bury the gold flakes. However, I am indebted to Lucius Beebe's 1946 *Stork Club Bar Book* for the following recipe for a layered cocktail (to be used only if you are sure your eggs are free of salmonella):
Golden Slipper: A measure of yellow Chartreuse is poured into a *copita* or sherry glass. A separated egg yolk is then dropped whole on to the surface of it, and a measure of Goldwasser carefully poured on top of that. (I haven't tried this. I suspect it may look rather prettier than it tastes.)

The commercial prototype of the drink was first made in the Baltic port city of Danzig (now Gdansk in Poland). Based on the drink kümmel, it is flavoured with both aniseed and caraway seeds and is colourless, less sweet than many liqueurs, and it really does have a shower of real golden particles added to it, in memory of Arnaldo. When the bottle was poured, the gold specks flurried up to general approbation like the flakes in a snowstorm toy. (There was also for a time a silver version, Silberwasser.) Liqueur d'Or was a now-extinct French version of the same thing. Some brands also had a citric fruit flavour – sometimes lemon, sometimes orange.

HOW TO SERVE
The prettiness can be enhanced by serving Goldwasser in a little cut-crystal liqueur glass.

TASTES GOOD WITH
Soufflé Rothschild is a very classical, hot dessert soufflé made from crème patissière and crystallized fruits that have been macerated in Danziger Goldwasser. It is served in individual soufflé dishes surrounded by strawberries.

GRAND MARNIER

GRAND MARNIER IS ONE of the best-loved of all the world's orange-flavoured liqueurs. The original product is a little younger than Cointreau, its big French rival, but the style is quite different. In the sense that the oranges used in it are bitter varieties from the Caribbean, it may be classed as another type of Curaçao, but it is a distinctly finer product than most ordinary Curaçao.

The house that owns it was founded in 1827 by a family called Lapostolle. Louis-Alexandre Marnier later married into the family business and it was he who, in 1880, first conceived the liqueur that bears his name. Encountering the bitter oranges of Haiti on a grand tour, he hit upon the idea of blending their flavour with that of finest cognac, and then giving it a period of barrel-ageing that basic Curaçao never receives.

Today, the production of the liqueur is split between two centres, one at Château de

GRAND
MARNIER
Fully the equal of
the higher grades
of cognac

FLAVOURING
Oranges

Bourg in the Cognac region, the other at Neauphle-le-Château, near Paris. The initial blending is carried out at the former site, the ageing at the latter. What results is a highly refined, mellow full-strength spirit that has a warm amber colour and an intense, festive scent of ripe oranges. It is sweet, but the distinction of the Fine Champagne cognac on which it is based prevents it from being in any way cloying when served straight.

The Marnier-Lapostolle company also decided to try cashing in on the mania for cream liqueurs that has arisen in the last 20 years or so by launching a Crème de Grand Marnier at much lower strength, which I can't find it in my heart to recommend.

HOW IT IS MADE
The juice of Caribbean oranges is blended with top-quality cognac. After full amalgamation of the flavours, it is then re-distilled, sweetened and given a period of cask-ageing.

TASTES GOOD WITH
It is the classic ingredient in duck à l'orange, and may also be used in a whole range of desserts, particularly flamed crêpes and anything made with strong chocolate.

HOW TO SERVE
As reverently as best cognac.

KAHLUA

K AHLÚA IS THE only liqueur of any note to
have been conceived in Mexico. It is a
dark brown coffee-flavoured essence packaged
in a round-shouldered, opaque bottle with a
colourful label. Although some of it is still
made in Mexico using home-grown coffee
beans, it is also made under licence in Europe
by the Danish company Peter Heering. It is
inevitably often compared to the other, more
famous coffee liqueur, Tia Maria, but it is
slightly thicker in texture and somewhat less
sweet than its Jamaican counterpart.

FLAVOURING
Coffee

KAHLUA
A liqueur with the
stimulant properties
of strong coffee

HOW TO SERVE
Kahlúa makes a very good chilled alternative
to a liqueur coffee. Pour the Kahlúa over
crushed ice in a tall glass and float some
thick cream on top. Alternatively, add it to
hot black coffee, top it with cream and a
dusting of ground cinnamon. Some think it
mixes well with either Coca-Cola or
milk as a long drink.

TASTES GOOD WITH
To enhance the flavour of a coffee dessert such
as a soufflé or ice cream, Kahlúa somehow
gives a smoother result than the more
commonly used Tia Maria.

IZARRA
Izarra is a sort of Basque version of
Chartreuse, made in Bayonne in southwest
France. It is flatteringly imitative to the
extent that it comes in two colours – yellow
and green – both full of aromatic herbs gathered wild in the Pyrenees. Green Izarra is
higher in alcoholic strength. (It is in fact, at
55%, exactly the same strength as green
Chartreuse, but doesn't really have the same
complexity of flavour.) The name means
"star" in the local dialect. Izarra is based on
armagnac, which is given a redistillation
with the aromatizing ingredients, followed
by a period of cask-ageing. Not surprisingly,
it is not much seen outside its native region.

MIXING
Black Russian: Certain
aficionados insist on
Kahlúa rather than Tia
Maria with the vodka.
Either way, it is as well
not to adulterate the
drink with cola.
Alexander the Great:
Shake a measure-and-a-
half of vodka with half
a measure each of
Kahlúa, crème de cacao
and thick cream and
plenty of ice. Strain into
a cocktail glass. (This
drink is reputed to have
been invented by the
great Nelson Eddy.)

KUMMEL

KUMMEL IS ONE of the more ancient liqueurs. All we know is that it originated somewhere in northern Europe, although we do not know exactly where. The best guess is Holland, but the Germans have a respectable enough claim on the patent as well (its name is, of course, German). Certainly, it was being made in Holland in the 1500s, and it very much fits the image of such drinks of the time, in that it would have been an unrefined grain spirit masked by an aromatic ingredient.

The ingredient in this case is caraway seeds. A certain amount of needless confusion is created by the fact that the name looks as though it has something to do with the more pungent cumin. This is only because, in certain European languages, caraway is often referred to as a sort of cumin. They have nothing to do with each other, the misleading nomenclature only arising because the seeds are supposed to look vaguely similar.

KUMMEL
Wolfschmidt is the leading brand of kümmel

MIXING
Tovarich: Shake a measure and a half of vodka, a measure of kümmel and the juice of half a lime with ice, and strain into a cocktail glass.

FLAVOURING
Caraway seeds

A key episode in kümmel's history occurred at the end of the 17th century, during Peter the Great's sojourn in Holland. He took the formula for the drink, to which he had grown rather partial, back to Russia with him, and kümmel came to be thought of as a Russian product, or at least as a Baltic one. The Baltic port of Riga, now capital of Latvia, was its chief centre of production throughout the 19th century, and some was also made in Danzig (now Gdansk), where they eventually came to add flecks of gold to it and call it Goldwasser.

Versions of kümmel are today made not just in Latvia but also in Poland, Germany, Holland, Denmark and even the United States. Not the least valued property of caraway, valued since Egyptian times, is its ability to counteract flatulence, which is why it was one of the traditional ingredients of gripe water for babies.

HOW IT IS MADE
The base is a pure grain distillate, effectively a type of vodka, in which the seeds are infused. Most brands are fairly heavily sweetened but they are always left colourless.

TASTES GOOD WITH
Try adding it to the mixture for old English seed cake, which is made with caraway seeds.

HOW TO SERVE
Kümmel is nearly always served on the rocks in its countries of origin.

LIQUEUR BRANDIES

SOME FRUIT LIQUEURS have traditionally been referred to as "brandies", even though they are properly nothing of the sort in the sense that we now understand that term. There are essentially three fruit brandies – cherry, apricot and peach – and, although they are occasionally known by other names, it is as cherry brandy, etc. that drinkers know them best.

Strictly speaking, these products belong to the same large category as those liqueurs prefixed with the phrase "crème de", in that they are sweetened, coloured drinks, based on simple grape brandy that has been flavoured with the relevant fruits, as opposed to being

FLAVOURINGS

Apricots
Cherries
Peaches

OTHER NAMES

France: Apricot brandy is sometimes known as Apry or Abricotine.
Liqueur brandies may eventually come to be known as apricot liqueur, etc. if the term "brandy" is enforced for grape distillates only. (The alternatives could well be crème d'abricot, de cerise and de pêche.)

MIXING

Paradise: Shake a measure of gin with half a measure each of apricot brandy and fresh orange juice and ice, and strain into a flared wine glass.

CHERRY BRANDY
Indispensable in the making of a Singapore Sling

HOW TO SERVE
The best of these liqueur brandies make wonderful digestifs served in small quantities, provided they are not the very sweetest styles.

primary distillates of those fruits themselves. The maceration of the fruit usually includes the stones or pips as well, for the bitter flavour they impart and – in the case of apricot kernels especially – the distinctive flavour of almond.

Of the three, the apricot variant has probably travelled the furthest. There are true apricot distillates made in eastern Europe, of which the Hungarian Barak Pálinka is the most renowned, but they are dry like the fruit brandies of France. Good examples of sweet apricot liqueurs are Bols Apricot Brandy, Cusenier and Apry made by the Marie Brizard company.

Cherry brandy is one of the few liqueurs that may just have been invented by the English, the role of creator being claimed by one Thomas Grant of Kent. The original version was made with black morellos, although other cherry varieties may be used in modern products, depending on what is locally available. English

cherry brandy contributed to the downfall of the dissolute King George IV, who consumed it in ruinous quantities, perhaps to get over the memory of his doomed affair with Mrs Fitzher-bert in Brighton.

Among the more famous cherry liqueur brands are Cherry Heering, now properly known as Peter Heering Cherry Liqueur, which was first formulated in the mid-19th century by a Danish distiller of that name. The Heering company grows its own cherries to make this product, which is cask-aged. Others include Cherry Rocher, de Kuyper, Garnier, and Bols, and there are brands produced in Germany and Switzerland.

Peach brandy is the one least frequently seen, its most famous manifestation probably being the one marketed by Bols.

HOW THEY ARE MADE

The pressed juice and stones of the respective fruits are generally mixed with a neutral grape spirit (more rarely a grain spirit), sweetened with sugar syrup and macerated until take-up of flavour is complete. If the fruit juice itself has fairly high natural sweetness, correspondingly less syrup will be added. In some cases, the liqueurs may be treated to a period of cask-ageing, followed by adjustment of the colour with vegetable dyes.

TASTES GOOD WITH

They all work well in fruit-based desserts that use the same fruits, for example hot soufflés, tarts and charlottes.

APRICOT BRANDY
Cusenier's liqueurs all come in these distinctive bottles

HEERING
Named after a Danish distiller in the last century.

MALIBU

FLAVOURING
Coconut

WITH THE GROWTH of tourism in the Caribbean islands, it was only a matter of time before liqueurs flavoured with coconut began to make their presence felt on the international market. Of these, the most famous is Malibu. Presented in an opaque white bottle, with a depiction of a tropical sunset on the front, it is a relatively low-strength blend of rectified Caribbean white rum with coconut extracts. The flavour is pleasingly not too sweet. Malibu was a better product than most of the range of liqueur concoctions with totally tropical names that bombarded the market during the cocktail renaissance of the early 1980s.

Another reasonably good product was Batida de Coco, a coconut-flavoured neutral spirit made in Brazil that was also exported in quantity to the holiday islands of the Caribbean. Cocoribe was similar.

They are all colourless products, with an alcohol level slightly higher than that of fortified wine. Since the success of these proprietary products, some of the famous Dutch and French liqueur manufacturers have got in on the act and also marketed variants of crème de coco.

HOW TO SERVE
These drinks are not great on their own, but make excellent mixes with ice and fruit juices, which is how they were intended to be served in the first place.

MIXING
Pina Colada: A sort of cheat's version can be made using Malibu instead of real coconut milk. Mix in equal measures with white rum and plenty of ice. Top up with pineapple juice.
Batida Banana: Mix equal measures of Batida de Coco with crème de banane and several ice-cubes in a tall glass. Top up with whole milk. (This is a dangerously moreish drink, effectively little more than a grown-up milkshake.)

HOW THEY ARE MADE
Most of the coconut liqueurs are based on ultra-refined white rum, although one or two are made with a neutral grain alcohol. The dried pulp and milk of the coconut are used to flavour the spirit, which is then sweetened and filtered.

TASTES GOOD WITH
A splash of coconut liqueur may productively be added to the sauces in Cajun or Far Eastern dishes, particularly those of Thai or Indonesian cuisine where coconut itself figures strongly. Otherwise, it is splendid as a flavouring in a richly creamy ice cream.

BATIDA DE COCO
Brazil's contribution to the coconut collection.

MALIBU
Perhaps the best of the coconut liqueurs

MANDARINE NAPOLEON

MANDARINE IS ANOTHER TYPE of Curaçao, this time made with the skins of tangerines as opposed to bitter Caribbean oranges. By far the most famous brand is Mandarine Napoléon, the origins of which really do derive from the drinking preferences of the Emperor Napoleon I. The key figure in its history is a French chemist, one Antoine-François de Fourcroy, who rose to prominence in France as a key figure in public administration after the Revolution.

Following the demise of the Jacobin regime, de Fourcroy found favour with Napoleon Bonaparte to the extent that he was made a member of his Imperial State Council. When the tangerine first arrived in Europe from China (hence its synonym, mandarine) at the end of the 18th century, there was something of a craze for it. The fashion was to steep the peel in cognac after eating the fruit, and Antoine-François records in his diary that many was the night he was called on to share in the Emperor's indulgence.

Mandarine Napoléon was launched in 1892 by a Belgian distiller, Louis Schmidt, who stumbled on the recipe in de Fourcroy's correspondence while pursuing some chemical

MANDARINE NAPOLEON
A French invention now made in Belgium

OTHER NAMES
France: Mandarine *Italy*: Mandarinetto

HOW TO SERVE
Despite its sweetness, it does work well as an after-dinner drink taken straight or *frappé* in a traditional brandy balloon.

FLAVOURING
Tangerines

researches. It was only after the Second World War, when the distillery was relocated from Belgium to France, that the Fourcroy family once again became involved, eventually taking on the worldwide distribution of Schmidt's liqueur. As it became ever more successful, they moved the production back to Brussels, where it remains.

The tangerines used in Mandarine come exclusively from Sicily. Other companies make versions of tangerine liqueurs – the Italians themselves of course make one from their Sicilian crop – but Mandarine Napoléon remains justifiably the pre-eminent example, a thoroughly individual product that has deservedly won international awards.

HOW IT IS MADE
For Mandarine Napoléon, tangerine skins are steeped in cognac and other French brandies. The spirit is then re-distilled, sweetened, coloured with carotene to a vivid yellowy-orange and matured for several months. It is bottled at 38% ABV.

TASTES GOOD WITH
Add it to tangerine-flavoured mousses or use it as the fuel to flame sweet pancakes.

MIXING
Titanic: Mix equal measures of vodka and Mandarine Napoléon over ice in a tumbler, and top up with soda water.

MARASCHINO

THE ORIGINAL MARASCHINO (which should be pronounced with a "sk" sound in the middle, not "sh") was a distilled liquor of some antiquity made from a sour red cherry variety. The Italian name for the cherry was Marasca, which grew only on the Dalmatian coast. When the Italian-speaking enclave of Dalmatia was incorporated into the then Yugoslavia, Italian production of maraschino was continued in the Veneto, where plantings of the Marasca cherry were established from cuttings.

Maraschino is a clear liqueur derived from an infusion of pressed cherry

FLAVOURING
Marasca cherries

MIXING
Tropical Cocktail: Shake equal measures of dry French vermouth, maraschino and white crème de cacao with a dash each of Angostura and orange bitters and plenty of ice. Strain into a wine glass.

skins in a cherry-stone distillate. (This secondary infusion is why maraschino should technically be considered a liqueur rather than a spirit, as distinct from Kirsch.) After further distillation to obtain a pure, clear spirit, it is aged, ideally for several years. It always remains colourless, and should have a pronounced bitter cherry aroma, backed up by the nuttiness of the cherry stones.

A number of Italian firms are especially associated with the production of maraschino, notably Luxardo (which traditionally sells its product in straw-covered flasks at a knee-trembling 50% ABV), the venerable Drioli company and Stock.

HOW IT IS MADE

The pomace of pressed cherries is infused over gentle heat in a cherry distillate for several months. It is then rectified and transferred to neutral maturation vessels, made either from a light wood such as ash or from glass. It is sweetened with sugar syrup and left to age for several years.

TASTES GOOD WITH

It is incomparable for soaking the sponge in a layered cake, or poured over fresh cherries and many other fruits, such as peaches or apricots.

HOW TO SERVE
The best grades of maraschino should be smooth enough to drink on their own, but the sweeter it is, the more recourse to the ice-bucket you may feel is necessary.

MARASCHINO
The traditional straw-covered bottle of Luxardo

MIDORI

An instant hit when it was launched in the early 1980s, Midori was another stroke of marketing genius from the giant Japanese drinks group, Suntory. Not content with its range of fine Scotch-style whiskies and classed-growth Bordeaux property, Château Lagrange, Suntory aimed for a slice of the cocktail action with this bright green liqueur in an idiosyncratic little bottle of textured glass.

The flavouring agent is melons,

MIDORI
Cornering the market in melon liqueurs

MIXING
Green Caribbean: Shake equal large measures of white rum and Midori with ice, strain into a tall glass and top up with soda water. Add a slice of lemon.

not a particularly common one in the liqueur world, but its vivid green colour is achieved by means of a dye. Indeed, its greenness is its principal sales pitch, since *midori* is the Japanese word for green. The colour is perhaps intended to evoke the skins of certain melon varieties, as opposed to the flesh that is actually used to flavour it. Having said that, Midori doesn't especially recall any melon variety; it is actually much closer to banana, in both aroma and taste. It is sweet and syrupy, and at the lower end of standard alcoholic strength for liqueurs.

TASTES GOOD WITH
It was seized on by chefs in some of the more adventurous restaurants for use in desserts that involve tropical fruit. Salads of mango, pineapple, melon, passion-fruit and so forth are perfect choices, although again, there is that unapologetic colour to contend with.

MERSIN
Mersin is a Turkish version of Curaçao, a colourless liqueur based on grape spirit and flavoured with oranges and herbs. It is commonly taken with a chaser of the fierce black coffee of Turkey.

FLAVOURING
Melon

HOW TO SERVE
Midori is much better mixed than served straight, when its flavour quickly cloys. It blends beautifully with iced fruit juices, notably orange, except that the resulting colour is horribly lurid. Lemonade may make a more visually appealing marriage, but a sweet mixer with a sweet liqueur is never a brilliant idea.

NUT LIQUEURS

THE NUT-FLAVOURED liqueurs deserve to be considered separately since they form quite a large sub-group. Drinks relying on coconut for their principal taste are dealt with elsewhere (see Malibu); the flavourings here are those of hazelnut, walnut and almond.

In their French manifestations, the first two of those are straightforward enough. They are named noisette and crème de noix, after the French words for hazelnut and walnut respectively. In the case of almonds, it all becomes a little more complicated, basically because certain fruit stones, such as those of apricots and cherries, have an almond-like taste. A liqueur that

OTHER NAMES
Almond liqueurs: Amaretto (Italian), Crème d'amandes (French)
Hazelnut liqueurs: Noisette (French)
Walnut liqueurs: Crème de noix (French), Nocino (Italian)

contains almonds themselves is called crème d'amandes. However, a liqueur called crème de noyau – "noyau" being the French for the stone in which the almond-like kernel of a fruit is encased – will contain no actual almonds, only an approximation of the flavour.

These are all brandy-based drinks in which the chopped nuts are

HOW TO SERVE
These drinks are quite commonly taken with crushed ice as a digestif in France. Alternatively, they may be iced, slightly watered – about the same amount of water as liqueur – and drunk as aperitifs. The tradition in France is for a sweet appetizer (with the obvious exception of champagne), as distinct from the drier British taste.

FRANGELICO
A branded liqueur done up to look like a monk

NOCINO
A strong walnut liqueur from Italy

steeped in a clear grape spirit and the resulting liqueur is clarified and bottled in a colourless state. The exception is crème de noyau, which more often than not has a faint pinkish hue if it has been made from cherry stones. They are all sweet, with fairly syrupy textures, and make invaluable additions to the cocktail repertoire.

Italy produces a range of nut-based liqueurs, too. There is the distinctive almond-flavoured Disaronno Amaretto, and also a walnut liqueur called Nocino. In the 1980s, a product called Frangelico was released. It was a delicate straw-coloured liqueur flavoured with hazelnuts and herbs, then dressed up in a faintly ridicu-lous dark brown bottle designed to look like a monk. The large brown plastic top represented his cowl, and around the gathered-in waist, a length of white cord was knotted. It looked like a particularly embarrass-ing tourist souvenir, but the liqueur itself turned out to be delicious, not too sweet, and with an intriguing range of flavours.

EAU DE NOIX
A rare French
walnut liqueur

MIXING

Pink Almond: Shake a measure of Scotch with half a measure each of crème de noyau, Kirsch, fresh lemon juice and orgeat (a non-alcoholic almond syrup) with ice, and strain into a cocktail glass. (If you can't get orgeat, double the quantity of noyau.)

Walnut Whip: Shake equal measures of cognac, crème de noix and thick cream with ice and strain into a cocktail glass.

Mad Monk (below): Shake a measure each of gin and Frangelico with the juice of half a lemon and ice. Strain into a wine glass and add a squirt of soda.

HOW THEY ARE MADE

The nuts are crumbled up and left to infuse with the base spirit before sweetening and fil-tration. They are bottled at the average liqueur strength, around 25%. In the case of the crème de noix of Gascony, the walnuts are beaten off the trees while still green, the spirit is sweet-ened with honey and subjected to a further distillation. For crème de noyau, fruit stones are the infusion agent. They are usually either cherry or apricot, but peach and even plum may also be used.

TASTE GOOD WITH

They work well with nutty desserts – anything using almond paste or praline – but also in a chocolate mousse, or drunk alongside a piece of rich, dark fruitcake. Frangelico served chilled makes an unlikely table-fellow for a piece of mature Stilton.

FLAVOURINGS
Almonds
Walnuts
Hazelnuts
Fruit stones
Honey (in the case of some crème de noix)

PARFAIT AMOUR

FLAVOURINGS
Lemons or other citrus
fruits (such as the
larger, shapeless citron
of Corsica)
Cloves
Cinnamon
Coriander seeds
Violets

HOW TO SERVE
It is best to serve
Parfait Amour
unmixed, or else
blended with
something colourless
such as lemonade, in
order not to interfere
with your beloved's
enjoyment of the
colour. It tastes better
chilled, although you
may feel that an
excessively cold drink
may numb the
erogenous zones, which
wouldn't do at all.

THE LONG ASSOCIATION of drinking with
seduction is celebrated in the name of
purple Parfait Amour, "perfect love". In the
18th century particularly, the use of alcohol in
amorous pursuits had less to do with getting
your intended too stupefied to know what they
were doing, than with stimulating the erotic
impulses with artful concoctions of spices and
flowers mixed with the alcohol.

Parfait Amour
liqueur is really
the only surviving
link to that noble
tradition. It is
almost certainly
Dutch in origin;
its name, as with
all such potions,

*PARFAIT
AMOUR*
*Indelibly
associated
with
romance*

is French because that was considered the
romantic language par excellence. As its
(added) colour would lead you to expect, it is
subtly scented with violets, but the flavour
owes more to fruits and spices than flowers,
which marks it out quite distinctly from the
colourless crème de violette. The main components are citrus fruits – usually lemons – and a
mixture of cloves and other spices.

The drink enjoyed great popularity during the
cocktail boom in the 1920s. Apart from anything else, no other liqueur is quite the same
colour. There was once a red version of it too,
but somehow purple has come to be more inextricably associated with passion. Today, Parfait
Amour is made not only by the Dutch liqueur
specialists Bols, but by certain French companies as well.

HOW IT IS MADE
The various aromatizing elements are macerated in grape spirit, which may then be
re-distilled, and the purple colour is achieved
by means of a vegetable dye.

TASTES GOOD WITH
What else but a box of violet creams?

PASTIS

PASTIS IS ONE OF the most important traditional drinks of Europe, despite having only minority status in Britain and the other northern countries. Around the Mediterranean fringe of Europe, from southeast France to the Greek islands, in its various derivatives, pastis functions in the same thirst-quenching way as beer does further north. It is important in terms of the quantity consumed locally, and is of great cultural significance too. It is an in-between-times drink rather than just an aperitif; it's a drink for lazy afternoons watching *boules* being played in the village square. There is also the tradition of illicit home distillation.

Drinkers the world

OTHER NAMES
France: pastis *Greece*: ouzo *Spain*: ojen

MIXING
Monkey Gland: Shake two measures of gin with a measure of fresh orange juice and three dashes each of pastis and grenadine and plenty of ice, and strain into a large wine glass.

RICARD
The famous
pastis
of southern
France

over have, on first contact with pastis, usually been fascinated by its most famous property – namely, that it clouds up when mixed with water. This attribute, indeed, is what gives the drink its name, *pastis* being an old southern French dialect word meaning muddled, hazy or unclear.

PERNOD AND ABSINTHE
The very close similarities of pastis to anis have been noted elsewhere (see Anis). Depending on which authority you consult, the principal flavouring element in pastis is either liquorice or aniseed – perhaps more often the former – but there are other herbal ingredients in it as well. A neutral, highly rectified alcohol base, generally of vegetable origin, provides the background for the aromatizing agents, which are steeped in it before essence of liquorice or anise is added and the whole mélange is sweetened and diluted.

Aniseed has been known as a digestive aid in medicine since the time of the Egyptians, which is why, to this day, many over-the-counter stomach-settling remedies contain a hint of its flavour. (Oxyboldene, a popular French brand, is a case in point.) The history of pastis is somewhat entangled, however, with a similar type of drink that came to be seen as anything but health-giving. By the beginning of the 20th century, the name of absinthe was mud.

Apart from home distillates, and excepting individual brands, the only category of drink that has ever become extinct is absinthe. It was considerably stronger than much of today's commercial pastis, but what really doomed it was that it contained wormwood in concentrations that were held responsible for poisoning the brains of those who habitually drank it. During the late 19th century, absinthe became known as the house drink of decadent Parisian artists, Symbolist poets and others, many of whom died the kinds of squalid deaths associated with laudanum use during the English Romantic period 60 and 70 years earlier.

When absinthe was given its marching orders in France by a governmental decree of 1915, other countries soon followed suit. One of its chief manufacturers – the firm of Henri Pernod, which had been making it for over a century – then turned to making a similar product without wormwood at lower alcoholic strength, and using anise as its main flavouring agent. In effect, Pernod was the sanitized version of absinthe. The reissued edition of that great reference work, *The Savoy Cocktail Book*,

MIXING
Yellow Parrot: Shake equal measure of pastis, yellow Chartreuse and apricot brandy with ice, and strain into a cocktail glass over crushed ice.

PERNOD
Ricard's
northern
French
counterpart

HOW TO SERVE
Pastis should ideally be served in a small, thick-bottomed glass with about the equivalent amount of water. The water should be very cold, so as to obviate the need for ice. Those with slightly sweeter tastes may add sugar to it. The best way to do this is to balance a perforated spoon or metal tea-strainer with a sugar-cube on it across the top of the glass and then pour the water over it. (This was the traditional way to sweeten absinthe.)

MIXING
Bunny Hug: Shake equal measures of gin, Scotch whisky and pastis and strain into a cocktail glass. (Not for the novice cocktail drinker, this one.)

specifically recommends using Pernod as a substitute in those of its recipes that originally called for absinthe.

Pernod is perhaps the most familiar pastis on the market today. The other main French brand, Ricard, is now part of the same group, although they are made at opposite ends of France. Berger is the other company of note making this sort of product. In northern European countries, where there is often an ambivalence about the flavour of aniseed or liquorice in a drink, Pernod and Ricard have been much favoured as bases for a fruit-juice mixer, but the only unimpeachably authentic way to drink them in their native regions, particularly around the town of Marseilles, is diluted with a small quantity of water.

Somewhat unexpectedly, absinthe has made a cautious comeback in certain European countries, notably Switzerland and Portugal. Presumably it contains considerably less wormwood and therefore is only vaguely comparable to the real thing. A theory has gained currency that it was really only banned because it was

highly alcoholic (in which case the hallowed Chartreuse might have been expected to find itself in more difficulties than it has). A scientific writer, Harold McGee, points out that wormwood contains a toxic oil called thujone, which was almost certainly linked to the formation of lesions on the cerebral cortex of the recklessly heavy user. You pays your money…

SPAIN
The Spanish equivalent is *ojen* (pronounced "oh-hen"). It is named after the town where it is made and is sold in two versions: sweet and dry.

MIXING
In northern Europe and the United States, pastis is more often mixed with fruit juices. Its colourlessness makes it a useful base: sharper flavours such as grapefruit are the most successful. A fashion for drinking it with blackcurrant cordial was quite the thing in Britain in the 70s. It perhaps reminded the drinker of a certain type of childhood boiled sweet with a chewy centre that combined the flavours of liquorice and blackcurrant. **Pernod-and-black** topped up with sweet cider – known in the bars of the north of England as **Red Witch** – was a popular way of achieving oblivion in my own mis-spent youth.

FLAVOURINGS
Liquorice
Aniseed

MIXING
If you come across absinthe, and are feeling daring, this was the recipe for the original **Absinthe Cocktail**: Shake equal measures of absinthe and water with a dash of sugar syrup, a dash of Angostura and ice, and strain into a cocktail glass.

GREECE

After pastis, the most familiar relative of this family of drinks is Greek ouzo, much beloved of holidaymakers on the Peloponnese and the islands, perhaps even more so than retsina. The flavouring agent is anise and, like pastis, the drink turns milky-white when water is added. It is drunk in much the same way, except perhaps with somewhat more water than is common in France, and generally as an aperitif. The bottled strength is around 35–40% ABV, again similar to pastis.

FLAVOURINGS
Herbs – possibly including coriander, camomile, parsley, veronica (which was once used in France as a substitute for tea), even spinach!

HOW TO SERVE
Ouzo should be served cold in a small, thick-bottomed glass, either on its own, with about the equivalent amount of water, or with an ice cube or two.

OUZO
The drink of the sunny Greek islands

MIXING
Cocktails that include pastis tend to be among the most dramatic in the repertoire. Many of these contain no non-alcoholic ingredients. That is because a relatively small amount of pastis will have plenty to say for itself in even the most ferocious of mixes, concoctions that would drown the presence of many of the more delicate liqueurs.

Block and Fall: Stir together a measure each of cognac and Cointreau with half a measure each of pastis and calvados, over ice, in a tumbler.

Hurricane: Shake a measure and a half of cognac with half a measure each of pastis and vodka and ice, then strain into a cocktail glass.

Ojen Cocktail: Shake a double measure of dry ojen with a teaspoon of sugar, half a measure of water, a dash of orange bitters and ice, and strain into a small tumbler.

HOW THEY ARE MADE
The various herbs and plants are usually infused in a straight, highly purified vegetable spirit base and essence of anise or liquorice added. Further blending with rectified alcohol is followed by sweetening, and the drink is bottled at an average 35% ABV.

TASTES GOOD WITH
The combination of aromatizers in pastis is a particularly successful one with fish, either for marinating or adding to a sauce. Try marinating chunks of tuna in olive oil, pastis and dill and then grilling them on skewers.

PIMM'S

FOREVER ASSOCIATED with the English summer, Pimm's No. 1 Cup is a proprietary version of a fruit cup created by the eponymous Mr Pimm in the 1820s. James Pimm originally devised his recipe in order to mark out his own establishment in the City of London from the run of common-or-garden oyster bars – oysters being not much more than ten a penny in those days – which traditionally served stout ale to wash the bivalves down.

He did such a roaring trade with his fruit cup that Pimm began to market it ready-mixed in 1859, the asking price for a bottle being a stiffish three shillings. Since that time, Pimm's has gone through a number of owners, including – at the turn of the century – the then Lord Mayor of London, Sir Horatio Davies. Popular throughout the British Empire during colonial times, it came to enjoy a sudden vogue in France and Italy after the war.

In the early years of the 20th century, Pimm's was elaborated into six different versions, each based on a different spirit. The market has since whittled these down to just two, Pimm's Vodka Cup and the original – still sold as No. 1 Cup, and based on London gin, with an unmixed strength of 25% ABV. Pimm's has suffered somewhat from being seen as too fiddly to prepare. Its present owner, one of Britain's biggest drinks companies, has tried to combat that by launching little cans of pre-mixed Pimm's.

TASTES GOOD WITH

Classic English picnic foods – cucumber sandwiches, hard-boiled quail's eggs, crackers with cream cheese and crudités – are all made the more splendid with plenty of Pimm's. Take a big jug and throw in half a bottle of Pimm's and a litre of lemonade.

FLAVOURINGS

All highly secret of course, but it contains fruit extracts – notably orange – and at least one other alcoholic ingredient, perhaps Curaçao. Who knows?

HOW TO SERVE

A generous measure of Pimm's No. 1 should be poured over ice in a tall glass. (In Mr Pimm's oyster bar, they knocked it back by the pint). It is then topped up with lemonade or soda, and garnished with slices of orange, lemon and lime, a wedge of apple and a dangling twist of pared cucumber rind. If you can find fresh borage, use some of its smaller leaves instead of the cucumber. Float a little bundle of mint leaves on top. If that sounds too much of a fandango, just throw in a slice of lemon and get on with it.

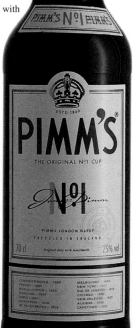

*PIMM'S
The quintessential flavour of an English summer*

POIRE WILLIAM

POIRE WILLIAM IS NOT to be confused with true pear brandy, which is a colourless spirit, eau de vie de poire, made in Alsace and Switzerland. The big liqueur companies nearly all make a sweet pear-flavoured liqueur, traditionally lightly coloured and made by the usual method of infusing crushed fruit in neutral grape spirit. Some may have a brief period of cask-ageing, but most don't.

One of the curiosities of Poire William – which is so named after the particular variety of pear used – is that, while its aroma is very strong and evocative, the flavour is often disappointingly mild. This is true of pears generally. The Williams is a gorgeously aromatic fruit when fully ripe but, used in cooking, its flavour often all but vanishes, which isn't at all true of the best apple varieties. As such, I find the liqueur has to be used in fairly enthusiastic quantities in a cocktail in order to get the best out of it.

Pear-flavoured liqueurs are made in France (about the best brand is Marie Brizard), Italy (which has Pera Segnana), Germany and Switzerland. A novelty product is Poire Prisonnière, which comes with a whole pear in the bottle. I remember as a student seeing one in a shop window in Venice and debating with a friend how on earth they managed to get the pear in. We eventually concluded they must somehow hand-blow the bottle around the fruit. So much for

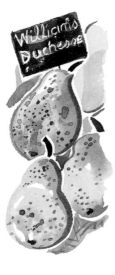

HOW TO SERVE
Served well-chilled, or perhaps with a single piece of ice, it makes a good aperitif. Alternatively, add a splash of lemonade.

MIXING
Old William (from G. Marcialis and F. Zingales's *Cocktail Book*): Pour a double measure of Poire William over ice in a tumbler. Add a half-measure each of maraschino and fresh orange and lemon juices, and mix thoroughly. Decorate with orange and lemon slices.

youthful ingenuity. The pears are in fact *grown* in the bottles, which are attached to the tree, so that each fruit has its own private greenhouse. Before the bottles are filled with the liqueur, the pears are pricked in order to release their juices.

TASTES GOOD WITH
Poire William is excellent poured over certain fresh fruits, notably pink grapefruit segments, pineapple or, of course, pear.

POIRE
WILLIAM
Delicately
flavoured
French pear
liqueur

POIRE
PRISONNIERE
The pear is
painstakingly grown
in the bottle

PUNSCH

PUNSCH IS MORE FAMILIARLY known in English-speaking countries as Swedish punch, although even then it isn't a drink many people have come across. Its lineage can be traced back to the 18th century, when Sweden's ocean-going trading vessels began doing business in the East Indies. Among the commodities they brought back was some of the arak that is the traditional spirit of those regions. Some arak is rice-based, some a distillate of sugar-cane, and therefore more like rum.

In its raw state, it wasn't much to northern European tastes, and so a few drink companies took to blending it with grape brandy and various wines and cordials, in effect creating a kind of powerful punch in the process. Like a traditional punch, the mixture is also highly spiced – just what the doctor ordered in the depths of the grim Scandinavian winter.

The original punch was a British colonial invention, but by the 18th century, a vogue for it had spread not only to

PUNSCH
The real thing – a cask-aged punsch from Sweden

OTHER NAMES
Britain: Swedish punch

MIXING
Diki-Diki: Shake a double measure of calvados, half a measure each of punsch and grapefruit juice, with ice, and strain into a cocktail glass.
Grand Slam (below): Mix a double measure of punsch with a measure each of dry white and sweet red vermouth, with ice, in a jug, and then strain over crushed ice in a wine glass.

Scandinavia but into France as well. Rum was a favoured base ingredient, variously boosted with hot tea, lemon juice and sweet spices such as cinnamon. Punch was, in every way, the grand-daddy of the cocktail.

In an echo of the British habit, Swedish punch was usually served hot, at least until the end of the last century. Since that time, the universal fashion for alcoholic drinks to be served cold has meant it is now drunk straight or even iced.

HOW IT IS MADE
These days, punch is exclusively a rum-based drink, to which other forms of alcohol – including wine – are added, together with a quantity of fragrant spices, such as cinnamon and cloves. It is sweetened and then aged for several months in cask.

TASTES GOOD WITH
Punch works reasonably well with little salty nibbles made with strong cheese.

FLAVOURINGS
Sweet spices, such as cinnamon and cloves

HOW TO SERVE
To relive the old days, warm the punsch gently (without letting it boil) in a small saucepan and serve it in big, heatproof, wine glasses.

RATAFIA

OTHER NAMES
France: Pineau des
Charentes (Cognac),
Floc de Gascogne
(Armagnac),
Pommeau (Calvados)

Rᴀᴛᴀғɪᴀ ᴡᴀs, ᴄᴇɴᴛᴜʀɪᴇs ᴀɢᴏ, a forerunner of the liqueur, in that it involved steeping fruits or nuts in a sweetened spirit base. That wouldn't in itself earn it a separate entry in this guide, were it not for the fact that the term ratafia has come to be applied mainly now to a type of aperitif made in the brandy-producing areas of France. The brandy is mixed with fresh fruit juice.

Ratafia is not a geographical name. It derives from the old French practice of concluding any formal agreement, such a legal contract or business transaction, with a shared drink – a "ratifier", if you like. The original phrase is Latin: *rata fiat* ("let the deal be settled").

There are also ratafias made in wine areas – particularly Burgundy and Champagne – in which the naturally sweet grape juice is mixed in with some of the regional wine. The most celebrated ratafia, however, is Pineau des Charentes, made in the Cognac region from grape juice fortified with cognac. It can't be considered a fortified wine, though, for

the very good reason that the grape juice has not undergone fermentation. It comes in white and rosé versions, and always has the sweetness of ripe grape juice about it.

In Armagnac, not to be outdone, they make their own version of this drink by exactly the same method. Called Floc de Gascogne, its production – like that of armagnac itself – is on a much more modest commercial footing than its Charentais counterpart.

There is also a variant of this type of ratafia made in the Calvados region of Normandy, in which fresh apple juice is fortified with apple brandy. It is called pommeau, and is a considerably more palatable proposition (to the author's taste at least) than either Pineau or Floc.

HOW IT IS MADE
By adding grape brandy to unfermented grape juice, or conversely apple brandy to apple juice, in each case to an average bottled strength of around 17% ABV.

TASTES GOOD WITH
Ratafia works quite well as an accompaniment to a slice of aromatic melon – better than most wine, at any rate.

HOW TO SERVE
These drinks should be served, vigorously chilled, in wine-glass quantities as aperitifs. In Armagnac, they mix the Floc with sparkling wine and call it a *pousse-rapière* (literally "rapier-pusher").

PINEAU DES CHARENTES
The ratafia of the Cognac region

POMMEAU
An apple ratafia from Normandy

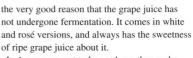

SAMBUCA

AN ITALIAN LIQUEUR that became quite
fashionable beyond its home region of
Rome in the 1970s and 80s, Sambuca Romana
is a clear, moderately sweet, quite fiery drink,
flavoured with elderberries and aniseed. Its
name is derived from the botanical name for
elderberry, *Sambucus nigra*. There are other
herbs and roots in it too, but these are the two
predominant flavours.

In the days when every drink had to be dignified with its own particular serving ritual, it was
decreed that Sambuca was to be garnished with
coffee beans and set alight. Aficionados of the
custom differed quite sharply as to whether the
correct number of beans was two or three. Such
detail scarcely mattered since what mostly
preoccupied the drinker was how to swallow it
without singeing the nose.

To earn your Sambuca stripes, you have to
blow out the flame on a glassful and then
swallow the drink in one, like an oyster. In
Rome, they will ask you whether you want it
con la mosca, literally "with a fly" (i.e. with the
coffee beans). There, they are not merely for
garnish. If you say *si*, you will be expected to
crunch the beans up as you drink.

SABRA

This is Israel's entry in the spirits and
liqueurs stakes – a svelte concoction
flavoured with a clever mélange of Jaffa
orange and chocolate. Despite the bitterness
contributed by the orange peels, the resulting
drink is exceptionally sweet. Try mixing it
with cognac and ice to throw it into relief.

MIXING

Matinée (from Michael Walker's *Cinzano
Cocktail Book*): Shake a measure of gin,
half a measure each of Sambuca and thick
cream, half an egg white and a dash of
fresh lime juice with plenty of ice, and strain
into a cocktail glass. Sprinkle with finely
grated nutmeg.

TASTES GOOD WITH

A chilled glass of
Sambuca makes a good
accompaniment to a
genuine Italian *torta*,
one of those heavenly
sticky cakes of dried
fruits, almonds and
lemon zest.

SAMBUCA
*A fiery liqueur
in more ways
than one*

FLAVOURINGS

Elderberries
Aniseed

HOW TO SERVE

If you are going to try
the flaming Sambuca
trick, it helps to serve
the liqueur in a narrow
glass like an old-
fashioned sherry
schooner, because the
flame will take more
easily on a smaller
surface.

SLOE GIN

SLOE GIN, AND its French equivalent *prunelle*, rely for their flavour and colour on a type of small bitter-tasting plum, the fruit of a shrub called the blackthorn. English sloe gin, as marketed by companies such as Hawker's, is nothing more than sweetened gin in which sloes have been steeped and then strained out once they have stained the spirit a deep red. The fruits contribute a strong, rather medicinal taste to the drink.

Prunelle, from the French word for the fruit, is not red but green, and is made by macerating the fruit kernels in a grape spirit base. Although the colour may be added, it does reflect the greenish flesh of the fruit. Liqueur companies such as Garnier and Cusenier (theirs is called Prunellia) make it, and it is especially popular in Anjou, in the western part

of the Loire valley. They also make eau de vie from sloes in Burgundy and Alsace.

The plant itself is a wild shrub that grows quite plentifully throughout Europe, its little sour fruits only ripening properly in early winter. Sloe gin is still quite widely made at home in country areas of England, but only with commercial gin, of course.

HOW IT IS MADE

Sloe gin is easy to knock up at home if you have access to the fruits. The best ratio is about half-a-pound of sugar to a pound of the fruit, but if the fruit is very sour, you may want to increase the sweetening by a couple of ounces. The fruit should be partly squashed or pierced to encourage absorption of the flavour. Top up your bottle with gin (or vodka, if you prefer, but gin makes a more interesting marriage of flavours). Leave it sealed for at least three months, shaking it up from time to time, and then strain the spirit off the solids.

TASTES GOOD WITH

Like cranberries or rowanberries, sloes make a good, tart jelly for garnishing strong gamey meats. Perhaps a slug of sloe gin in the sauce or gravy would help matters along.

HOW TO SERVE
Sloe gin is best served as it comes and at room temperature. A marketing push for a brand of sloe gin a few years ago suggested adding a teaspoon or two of it to a glass of sparkling wine, which isn't a bad idea – especially if the sparkling wine is a bit rough.

FLAVOURING
The fruit of the wild blackthorn bush

SLOE GIN
A sloe gin from one of the big names in gin

SOUTHERN COMFORT

THE FOREMOST AMERICAN liqueur is Southern Comfort, a fruitier counterpart to the Scotch-based liqueurs. Naturally American whiskey is used as its starting point. As so often in the world of proprietary liqueurs, the exact composition of Southern Comfort is a closely guarded commercial secret, but what we do know is that the fruit flavouring it contains is peach.

Its origins probably lie in the mixing of bourbon with peach juice as a traditional cocktail in the southern states. Back in Mississippi, down in New Orleans (as the song goes), there was once a mixed drink called Sazerac. A recipe for it is given in the *Savoy Cocktail Book*. It consists of a shot of rye

SOUTHERN COMFORT
A fruity whiskey liqueur of the Deep South

FLAVOURING
Peaches

whiskey, with a sprinkling of peach bitters, a lump of sugar and a dash of absinthe. So traditional is it that a New Orleans company has been producing a pre-mixed version of it since around the middle of the 19th century.

Peaches themselves are grown in great quantities in the southern states; the Georgia peach is one of America's proudest agricultural products. The practice of blending the peach juice with whiskey in the bars of New Orleans undoubtedly also played its part in influencing the creation of Southern Comfort.

Today, the company that owns the brand is the same one that has the leading Tennessee whiskey brand, Jack Daniel's. The Southern Comfort distillery is located in St Louis, in the state of Missouri. The bottled strength is high – 40% ABV – which is perhaps one of the reasons it appealed so much to the late great rock legend Janis Joplin.

TASTES GOOD WITH

Southern Comfort makes a good substitute for bourbon poured over the traditional light fruit-cake at Thanksgiving or Christmas. Quantities should be extremely generous, though: a whole bottleful is not unknown.

HOW TO SERVE
Southern Comfort is intended to be meditatively sipped, like other fine American whiskeys, but you could try taming its fire and emphasizing its fruitiness with a mixer of peach nectar. It's also fine with orange juice on the rocks.

STREGA

THE NAME STREGA, a popular proprietary liqueur produced in Italy, is Italian for "witch". It is so called because it is supposedly based on a witches' brew, an aphrodisiac love-potion guaranteed to unite any pair of lovers who drink it in eternal togetherness. You have been warned.

It is a bright yellow concoction full of all sorts of complex flavours. The fruit base is a citrus blend and it reputedly also contains around six dozen different botanical herbs, making it not dissimilar in style to the yellow version of Chartreuse. It has

the same kind of syrupy texture, too, and is considered an especially good digestif.

Although the colour resembles that other Italian liqueur speciality, Galliano, Strega's flavour is quite different, more obviously herbal and with a stronger citrus element.

TASTES GOOD WITH

As an accompaniment to freshly cracked nuts at the end of a meal, Strega works particularly well.

STREGA
This Italian liqueur is full of complex flavours

HOW TO SERVE
Strega is more appealing served *frappé*, on crushed ice, which takes the edge off its sweetness, than served on its own.

SUZE

IF I HAD TO NOMINATE one other product to make up a perfect trinity of aperitifs with champagne and pale dry sherry, it would unhesitatingly be Suze. Some may consider that Suze, and the various related Swiss and German products, should technically be considered under "Bitters", but they are not always direct distillates; some are actually wine-based. What they do all have in common is that they rely for their impact on gentian.

Gentian is a wild mountain plant found in the Alps and the mountains of the Jura, in France. It has large yellow flowers, but it is principally valued for its roots, which can grow up to a yard long and have one of the most uncompromisingly bitter flavours found anywhere in the plant world. It was once the quinine of its day, before that plant was brought back from the Americas in the 17th century. Like quinine, gentian has had a distinguished history in the pharmacist's repertoire; it was thought to be particularly good for ailments of the liver.

The Suze brand is owned by pastis manufacturers Pernod-Ricard, and it has a very

SUZE
Well worth a journey to France to taste

OTHER NAMES
France: Gentiane *Germany*: Enzian

MIXING
Drought: Shake equal measures of gin and Suze with a small splash of fresh orange juice, and strain into a cocktail glass. (This is an unimaginably dry mixture, and a particular energizer to the appetite.)

delicate primrose colour. It is based on wine, and its flavour is so dry and bitter, even when mixed with a little water or served on ice, that it acts as an extraordinarily powerful appetite-rouser.

Other similar products may be labelled Gentiane in France and Switzerland, or Enzian in Germany. The German products tend to be direct distillates of the gentian root, though, rather than wine-based.

HOW IT IS MADE
In the case of Suze and similar products, an extract of gentian is steeped in a white wine base, which imparts a little faint colour to the liquid. It is then clarified and bottled at fortified wine strength.

TASTES GOOD WITH
Suze is great served with any bitter nibbles, and is extremely appetizing with the more pungent varieties of green olive.

HOW TO SERVE
Pour a measure of Suze into a tumbler with either the merest splash of very cold water or a single cube of ice just to freshen it up.

FLAVOURING
Gentian root

GENTIANE
An alternative French brand of gentian aperitif.

TIA MARIA

JAMAICA'S CONTRIBUTION to the world of liqueurs, Tia Maria, has turned into one of the best-loved of all such products in both America and Europe. It is a suave, deep brown coffee-flavoured drink that proves itself highly versatile on the cocktail circuit as well as for after-dinner sipping.

It is based, not surprisingly, on good dark Jamaican rum of at least five-year-old standard and flavoured with the beans of the highly prized coffee variety, Blue Mountain. In addition to the coffee, the palate is further deepened by the addition of local spices too. Although the liqueur is sweet, noticeably sweeter than its Mexican counterpart Kahlúa, for example, the aromatic components in it prevent it from being cloying. This makes it one of the few such drinks that is actually quite acceptable to savour on its own.

Not the least reason for its popularity in Europe was the craze for the cocktail Black Russian, usually taken with Coca-Cola, in

FLAVOURINGS
Coffee
Spices

TIA MARIA
The world's most
famous coffee liqueur

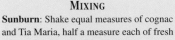

HOW TO SERVE
On the rocks is a pleasant way to serve Tia Maria as a digestif. Otherwise, it is one of the few liqueurs to make a truly appetizing mix with cola. Some like it with orange juice, but the resulting muddy colour is somewhat unlovely.

MIXING
Sunburn: Shake equal measures of cognac and Tia Maria, half a measure each of fresh orange and lemon juices and ice, and strain into a cocktail glass.
Proportions of the classic **Black Russian** (below) vary according to taste. Two parts vodka to one part Tia Maria on ice, with no mixer, makes a very adult drink.

which it provides a luxurious note of richness to what is otherwise a fairly prosaic mix.

HOW IT IS MADE
Coffee beans and spices are infused in a base of cask-aged rum, which is then lightly sweetened. It is bottled at just under 27% ABV.

TASTES GOOD WITH
Tia Maria is brilliant for lacing chocolate desserts, and of course makes a good liqueur coffee – particularly when the coffee used is Blue Mountain.

TRAPPISTINE
Another of the few remaining liqueurs made by religious orders, Trappistine is made at the convent of the Abbaye de Grâce de Dieu in the eastern French *département* of Doubs, not far from the Swiss border. A naturally pallid, yellow-green colour, it is based on armagnac and contains macerations of many wild herbs.

VAN *der* HUM

VAN DER HUM IS SOUTH AFRICA'S equivalent of Curaçao, made by several producers in the Cape, including the giant national wine consortium KWV. The whimsical name literally translates as "What's-his-Name". Its base is Cape brandy, of which there is a large annual production, and the citrus fruit used is a tangerine-like orange variety locally known as *naartjies*. Much in the way of Curaçao, the peels of the orange are infused in the brandy and supplemented with a herb or spice element. The precise formula may vary from one producer to the next, but nutmeg is a favoured addition.

Rather like Mandarine Napoléon, the drink derives from the practice of steeping citrus peels in the local brandy. Such a concoction would have been widely produced domestically by early Cape settlers, and the formula came to be replicated on a commercial scale. It is a reliable and attractive liqueur, its pale gold colour and pronounced bitter orange scent adding to its appeal. The bottled strength is generally 25%-plus.

VAN DER HUM
South Africa's answer to orange Curaçao

LA VIEILLE CURE

The correct translation of this liqueur's name is "The Old Rectory", not – as it would seem – "The Old Cure". The mistranslation would be right on at least one score, though. It was once a golden potion made by the monastic order at the abbey of Cenons, near Bordeaux. It used over 50 different curative wild herbs macerated in blended brandies, and was very much a typical medieval alcohol remedy, first conceived in the days when distillation went hand in hand with the pharmacist's art. The flavour has been compared to that of Bénédictine. To enjoy it to the full, La Vieille Cure should be served neat and un-iced in small liqueur glasses. In the 1980s, the production passed into the hands of one of the large French drinks companies of the region, but the liqueur's manufacture should not be confused with the wine-producing château of the same name in Bordeaux.

VERVEINE

Verveine du Vélay, to give it its full title, is another of those liqueurs that models itself stylistically on Chartreuse, to the extent that it comes in green and yellow, with the green the stronger. It is a brandy-based herbal concoction made near Puy, in the Auvergne region of central France. Verveine is the French for verbena, a flowering herb whose leaves have been used in folk medicine for centuries as a restorative for the liver and also for neurological complaints. Its bitter flavour is apparent in the liqueur named after it (though there are other herbs in it too), the sharpness gentled with a little honey.

FLAVOURINGS
Naartjie peels
Nutmeg and other spice and herb aromatizers

FORTIFIED WINES

THE DRINK PRODUCTS in this final section are, technically speaking, wines. If they were wines pure and simple, however, they would have no place in a book dealing with spirits and liqueurs. These wines have one important difference from ordinary table wines, though. They have all been fortified, and what they are fortified with is spirit, grape spirit more often than not. In that respect, none of these types of wine could have existed before the discovery of distillation.

In most cases, the creation of the classic fortified wines was a chance discovery occasioned in the course of trying to find ways of preserving ordinary wines. It wasn't that some bright spark in Portugal once thought, "Let's add some brandy to our wines and see what they taste like". The addition of spirit was intended to keep wines from spoiling on the long and often arduous sea voyages they had to undergo to their customers abroad.

In the days when the chemistry of fermentation was much less thoroughly understood than it is now, wine was often shipped, in the barrel, in a microbiologically unstable state. It may have been that its fermentation had only been interrupted by a sudden drop in the cellar temperature, as opposed to having run its natural course. When such wines arrived

at their destinations, it was often found that they begun re-fermenting or, worse, that they would re-ferment *after* being bottled.

The yeasts that ferment in grape juice and result in the production of alcohol can only continue to do their work as long as there is enough natural sugar in the liquid for them to feed on, and as long as the amount of alcohol generated doesn't exceed a certain level – usually estimated in the range of 16–17% by volume (ABV). After that, they die off, and the wine becomes stable. If you add a healthy dose of brandy or other spirit to wine that has apparently finished fermenting (or to one that is still in the process of fermenting, for that matter), you raise the alcohol level to such a degree that the yeasts are killed off.

In addition to then having a stable

Left: The essential flor (yeast cells) growing on the surface of a barrel of fino sherry.

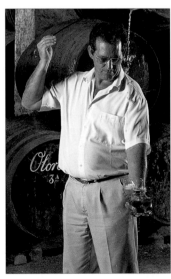

Above: For tasting, sherry is still taken from the barrels in the traditional way using a long handled venecia.

Left: Neat rows of vines and fermentation tanks bake in the hot sun in the Douro valley at Pinhao, Portugal.

wine on your hands, you also of course have a product that is a fair bit higher in alcohol than most ordinary wines. The normal strength of unfortified table wines is in the region of 11–13% ABV. Some German and Italian wines make a virtue of being particularly low in alcohol (as little as 5%, perhaps), while certain Italian and Californian wines made from grapes that have grown in raging hot climates may climb up to around 15%. But 15% is the *starting* point for fortified wines, and they can be fortified up to 22%, putting them not far off the strength of the average liqueur.

Each of the world's classic fortified wines (they originated in southern Europe, but are now made in most wine-making countries) has its own particular method of production. The majority are made from white grapes, the most

notable exception being port, most of which is red. They tend to be sweet, but don't have to be – fino and manzanilla sherry are the driest of the dry. Most of them contain only wine and grape spirit, but in the case of vermouth and related products, a whole bunch of aromatizing ingredients (familiar to us from some of the herbal liqueurs) creates a style that is halfway between a fortified wine and a liqueur.

Fortified wines may once have seemed a good way of using up a sub-standard harvest, either through the distillation of grapes to make the fortifying agent, or in masking a poor wine's faults by adding spirit to it. By the time the 19th century dawned, however, most of these wines were seen as premium products – vintage port and Madeira particularly were as highly acclaimed as claret and burgundy.

Above: At one time, on the Douro River, Porto, Portugal, small boats were used to bring barrels of port from high in the valley.

Until about the time of the Second World War, they were held in special regard by the British, who have always had a taste for strong and fiery wines. Since that time a progressive decline has taken place as international tastes in wine have tended to the dry and light end of the spectrum, and away from the sort of sinew-stiffening brew to be sipped by the fireside on winter nights.

Despite that, there will always be a place for the traditional fortified wines. In a world where table wine is often accused of being infected by a bland homogeneity of taste, the fortifieds are, in their several ways, unashamedly unique styles of wine.

MADEIRA

O F ALL THE CLASSIC fortified wines of southern Europe, Madeira is the one with the most singular history. It comes from the island of the same name in the Atlantic Ocean; a volcanic outcrop, Madeira is actually slightly nearer to the coast of North Africa than it is to Portugal of which it is an autonomously governed region.

The evolution of this wine belongs to the days of the trading ships that plied the East India routes in the late 1600s. Madeira's geographical position made it a natural port of call for north European vessels on their way to Africa and the East Indies, and so they would load up with wine at the port of Funchal, the island capital. It gradually came to be noticed that, whereas many table wines would be badly spoiled by the combination of violent

shaking and the torrid heat in which they travelled the oceans, Madeiras were eerily improved by the experience.

The shippers were so sure of the benefits the sea voyage conferred on the wine that they began to send wines that were only destined for the European markets all the way to Indonesia and back. Some went the other way, and a great connoisseurship of Madeira grew up in the newly independent United States. Until virtually the end of the 19th century, this is how the most highly prized Madeiras were all made.

Eventually, it simply wasn't financially practical to keep treating Madeira to a round-the-world cruise, and so the conditions it endured at sea – the tortuous heat, especially – were recreated in the wineries or "lodges" where the wines originated. Some Madeira is heated simply

VERDELHO
The second
driest style –
this 5-year-
old Madeira
is only very
slightly sweet

HOW TO SERVE
Serve Madeira in a good-sized sherry glass or small wine glass. The drier styles may benefit from a little light chilling, but the richer, darker styles, with their overtones of treacle toffee and Christmas cake, should be served at room temperature.

RICH
MALMSEY
This is the
sweetest style
of Madeira

MIXING

It was common in America once to substitute sweet Madeira for the brandy in a **Prairie Oyster**, that most challenging of hangover cures, involving a raw egg yolk, salt and cayenne pepper and a dash of Worcestershire sauce.

Boston (below): Shake equal measures of dry Madeira and bourbon with half a teaspoon of caster sugar and yet another egg yolk. Strain into a small wine glass and sprinkle with grated nutmeg.

by being left under the roof of the lodge to bake in the heat of the tropical sun. Some is stored in rooms where fat central heating pipes run around the walls throughout the summer swelter, and even the lowest grades are matured in vats that have hot-water pipes running through them.

There are four basic styles of Madeira, named after the grape varieties that go into them. The palest and driest style is Sercial. Then comes Verdelho, a little sweeter and darker, then Bual, and finally Malmsey (the last is an English corruption of the Portuguese name Malvasia). The wines are also graded according to how long they have been aged. This may be given as a minimum age on the label (5-year-old, 10-year-old and so on), or one of the accepted descriptive terms may be used. "Reserve" equates roughly to 5-year-old, "Special Reserve" to 10, "Extra Reserve" to 15. Some Madeira is vintage-dated, meaning it is the unblended produce of the stated year's harvest.

HOW IT IS MADE

A light, white base wine is made from any of the four main varieties, perhaps supplemented with some juice from the local red grape Tinta Negra Mole (though it is theoretically of declining importance). For the sweeter styles, Bual and Malmsey, the fermentation may be interrupted early on by the addition of grape spirit, meaning that some natural sugar remains in them, while the drier wines (Sercial and Verdelho) are fermented until more of the sugar has been consumed before being fortified. The wines are then subjected to heat during the cask-ageing, either by one of the heating systems known as an *estufa* (stove), or else by just being left in the hottest part of the lodge, in which case it may be known as a *vinho canteiro*.

SERCIAL
The palest and driest style of Madeira

TASTES GOOD WITH

The driest styles present the answer to that age-old problem of what to drink with soup. They are particularly good with clear, meaty consommé. As you proceed to the richer end of the scale, drink them with mince pies, Christmas cake and other dense fruitcake mixes or, of course, Madeira cake.

MARSALA

SICILY'S VERY OWN fortified wine is named after the town of Marsala, in the province of Trapani at the western end of the island. Like many of the fortified wines of southern Europe, it has an English connection. It was effectively invented by a wine merchant, John Woodhouse, in 1773, in direct imitation of the sherry and Madeira in which he was something of a specialist. In the rough-and-ready way of the time, he simply added a quantity of ordinary brandy to the traditional white wines of western Sicily, and found on shipping them that the result was a reasonably close approximation of the already established fortified wines.

Woodhouse founded a commercial operation on the island at the end of the 18th century, and won valuable orders from the Royal Navy among others. Marsala was carried on Nelson's ships during the hostilities with France, and the wine's reputation quickly spread. Although the early trade was dominated by English merchants, Italians themselves eventually got in on the act. The first significant house of Italian origin was Florio, founded by an entrepreneur from the mainland in 1832.

It is fair to say that Marsala's development since that period has been one of slow decline as a result of conflicting theories about how it should be made, and the widespread use of irrigation in the vineyards where it is grown. Irrigation can result in grapes of lower sugar concentration, which means that alternative methods of sweetening the wine have had to be found.

The rules and regulations governing the production of Marsala

HOW TO SERVE

Dry and medium-dry Marsala, of which there is a regrettably small amount, should be served chilled in generously sized sherry glasses as an aperitif.

The sweetest styles should be served at room temperature as digestifs or with certain types of old, dry cheese.

TERRE ARSE
A vintage-dated
Marsala from
Florio

SECCO
The driest style
of Marsala

MIXING

Casanova: Shake a measure of bourbon with half a measure each of sweet Marsala and Kahlúa, a measure of thick cream and plenty of ice. Strain into a cocktail glass.

Inigo Jones (from Michael Walker's *Cinzano Cocktail Book*): In a mixing-jug, stir together a measure of cognac, a measure of sweet Marsala, a measure of dry rosé wine and a dash each of fresh orange and lemon juices with plenty of ice. Strain into a tumbler half-filled with crushed ice.

HOW IT IS MADE

Light white wines from local grape varieties Grillo, Inzolia and Catarratto are turned into Marsala by one of three methods. They can be fortified with grape spirit in the traditional way, or sweetened and strengthened with either alcohol-boosted juice from ultra-sweet, late-ripened grapes or with cooked grape juice concentrate. Concentrate is only permitted in the Ambra Marsala. The wines are then cask-aged for varying periods.

TASTES GOOD WITH

Marsala has come to be seen as even more of a kitchen ingredient than Madeira. It is indispens-able as the alcohol element in both zabaglione and tiramisù, while the scallopini of veal, beloved of Italian trattorias the world over, are often sauced with a sticky brown reduction of Marsala.

DOLCE
This is best suited for classic Italian desserts

FINE

Fine Marsala is the youngest style

RISERVA

Superiore Riserva Marsala is four years old

were only finally codified in 1969, and are con-siderably more flexible than those controlling the manufacture of the other famous fortified wines. Perhaps the least satisfactory aspect of them is the nature of the sweetening agents that may be added. It can be either a fortified grape juice, or just grape juice whose sweetness has been concentrated by cooking. This latter ingre-dient, known in Italian as *mosto cotto*, is not in itself alcoholic. The best Marsalas have natural sweetness from ripe grapes, which is retained through interrupted fermentation.

Marsala is classified by age – Fine is one year old, Superiore two, Superiore Riserva four, Vergine five, Stravecchio ten – and by sweet-ness. Dry is labelled "secco", medium-dry "semisecco" and the sweetest "dolce". It also comes in three colours. The better grades are both shades of tawny, either amber (*ambra*) or golden (*oro*), but there is a red version too (*rubino*). Producers of note include de Bartoli, Pellegrino and Rallo.

MUSCAT *and* MOSCATEL

SWEET FORTIFIED WINES are made from Muscat all over the world. It is easy to think Muscat is a single grape variety, but it is in fact a grape family. Some of its offshoots are of the highest pedigree, notably a type the French call Muscat Blanc à Petits Grains. Others, such as Muscat of Alexandria and Muscat Ottonel, are of humbler extraction, and give corresponding-ly less exciting wines. Moscatel is the name the family assumes on the Iberian peninsula.

This is a quick global tour of the styles of sweet wine the Muscat relatives make. All should be served chilled as dessert wines or on their own. They tend to be in the range of 15–18% ABV, except for the first category, Australian Muscats, which reach up to 20%.

AUSTRALIAN LIQUEUR MUSCATS

These are hugely rich, strong, fortified Muscats made in and around the town of Rutherglen, in the north-western corner of the Australian state of Victoria. They are produced by a method that seems to combine a little of all the ways of making fortified wine. The grapes are left to overripen and shrivel on the vine, so that they are halfway to becoming raisins. After pressing, they ferment part-way, but the fermentation is arrested by fortification with grape spirit, keeping massive quantities of natural sugar in the wine. The cask-ageing they then receive combines elements of the *solera* system used in Spanish brandy and sherry, and the action of searing sunshine, as in *canteiro* Madeiras. Among the more notable producers are Stanton & Killeen, Mick Morris and Chambers.

VIN DOUX NATUREL MUSCATS

A group of Muscat wines made in southern France are made by virtually the same method as port. Their collective name, *vins doux naturels*, means "naturally sweet wines". The grapes are picked very ripe and the normal process of fermentation is stopped by adding a powerful grape spirit, so the natural grapey sweetness of Muscat is retained. There are six appellations for this type of wine, the most famous of which comes from the southern Rhône valley – Muscat de Beaumes de Venise. Best producers are Domaine Durban and Domaine de Coyeux.

Four of the others are located down in the Languedoc. They are Muscat de Frontignan, de Lunel, de Mireval and de St Jean de Minervois. The sixth, Muscat de Rivesaltes, is grown even further south, in Roussillon, near the Spanish border. De Rivesaltes does not have to be made from the noblest Muscat, though, and the quality varies hugely between producers.

SETUBAL MOSCATEL

This is a highly traditional fortified wine based on the Muscat of Alexandria grape, together with a couple of its more obscure cousins. It is made on the Setúbal peninsula in western Por-tugal, southeast of Lisbon, and was recognized

MUSCAT DE BEAUMES DE VENISE Domaine de Coyeux is one of the best producers of Muscat

as a regionally demarcated wine in the first decade of the 20th century. The process is the same as for the French *vins doux naturels*, except that after fortification, the grape skins are allowed to macerate in the finished wine for several months. Some Setúbal Moscatel is released after five years or so when its colour is already a vivid orange from the wood. Other wines are aged for a couple of decades, deepening to burnished mahogany until they are a treacle-thick essence of pure Muscat flavour. The most significant producer is José Maria da Fonseca.

MOSCATEL DE VALENCIA

Around Valencia, on the eastern coast of Spain, they make what the French would call a *vin de liqueur*, that is, a wine that hasn't

SETUBAL MOSCATEL

A 20-year-old Moscatel from Portugal's Setúbal

really fermented as such but for which the grapes have merely been pressed and then fortified with grape spirit. (In that respect, they could be considered similar to the ratafias made in the brandy regions of France.) Moscatels de Valencia are not made from the most distinguished Muscat variety and are more often than not seen in screw-top bottles. When very fresh and very well chilled, these can be pretty refreshing drinks, particularly in the stunning heat of a Spanish summer.

JEREPIGO

Jerepigo is the South African version of Moscatel de Valencia, except that it most emphatically does use the aristocratic Muscat Blanc à Petits Grains variety, here known – just to confuse everybody – as Muscadel or Muskadel. Otherwise, the production is the same, with grape spirit being added to the very sweet, freshly pressed grape juice. Vintages of Jerepigo (the name is Portuguese in origin) are occasionally released at around 15 years old, and are found to retain much of their initial freshness.

MOSCATEL DE VALENCIA

A highly ornate bottle for what is in fact a very simple drink

JEREPIGO

An old vintage of South Africa's answer to fortified Moscatel.

PORT

P ORT IS THE ONLY one of the major fortified
wines to be based on a red wine. True, there
is such a thing as white port, but it only
accounts for a fraction of the production. Port
hails from only one delimited area, the Douro
valley in northern Portugal. So popular has it
traditionally been as a style of wine that many
non-European wine-making countries have
been trying their hands at port lookalikes since
the 19th century. The difference today is that, in
the countries of the European Union at least,
they are no longer allowed to be called port.

The drink originated during one of the fre-
quent periods of hostilities between the English
and the French in the
1600s, as a consequence
of which the English
authorities declared a
punitive tax levy on
goods imported from

France. This hit the wine trade hard. Wine shippers had to look to Portugal, England's oldest
European ally, with whom there were preferen-
tial trade tariffs, to supply their customers.
Journeying inland along the river Douro, the
English merchants happened upon the fierce red
wines of the region and found them pretty much
to the domestic taste. As was common practice
at the time, they fortified them with a little
brandy for the sea voyage.

Thus was port born.
Originally, it was of
course a dry wine, since
these were fully fer-
mented wines that were
being augmented with
brandy. However, it
only took the chance
discovery of the
effects of fortification

COCKBURN'S
1991
A vintage port from
one of the English
shippers

GRAHAM'S
1989 LBV
Port from a single
year matured in the
shipper's cellars

HOW TO SERVE
Good port should be
served in wine-glass
quantities, not in silly
little liqueur glasses,
unchilled except in the
case of white port.
Older wines that have
thrown a sediment may
need to be decanted.

on an extremely ripe, sweet wine to remodel port in the image with which we are familiar today. To preserve that sweetness, the wines would have their normal fermentation interrupted (or "muted") with brandy, so that some of the grape sugars would remain unconsumed by the yeasts.

Eventually, it was considered that using a simple local grape spirit was cheaper than buying fine cognac for the fortification. Also, port was coming to be seen as a fine wine in its own right, and so it was desirable that the fortifying agent should be as neutral as possible, in order to allow the characteristics of the underlying wine to be shown off.

Port styles have since multiplied almost *ad infinitum*. At the top of the quality tree are the vintage ports, wines of a single year that must be bottled within two years of the harvest and are intended for long ageing. Late-bottled vintage (LBV) is also the product of a single year, but, one that has been kept in cask in the shipper's premises for longer – around six years usually – in order to be more mature on bottling, and readier to drink on purchase. Vintage Character port is an everyday blended product and nothing special, while the fine old tawny ports are often aged for many years in barrel so that their initial full-blooded red fades to an autumnal brown.

Other countries producing good port-style fortified wines are Australia (where the favoured grape variety is the spicy Shiraz), South Africa and the United States. There is a very good Greek fortified red called Mavrodaphne that makes an agreeable alternative to the more basic offerings of the Douro.

HOW IT IS MADE
The fermentation of Douro wines is stopped part-way through by the addition of grape spirit, to produce a sweet, strong, liquorous wine. Various periods of cask-ageing are given to the various grades. The bottled strength is in the region of 18-20%, but can be as high as 22%.

TASTES GOOD WITH
Port is excellent with nuts and with mature, strong hard cheeses, such as Cheddar, but less good with its traditional partner, Stilton.

TAYLOR'S 20 YEARS OLD
Twenty years is the average age of the blend

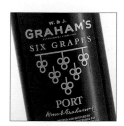

GRAHAM'S SIX GRAPES
A fairly basic ruby port

COCKBURN'S FINE RUBY
This is the lowest port designation

QUINTA DO CRASTO
An LBV from a small Portuguese producer

QUADY'S
A port-style fortified wine from the USA

SHERRY

ALTHOUGH FORTIFIED WINES bearing the name of sherry have been produced around the world for well over a century, true sherry comes only from a demarcated region in the southern Spanish province of Andalucía. There are three main centres of production – Jerez de la Frontera, Puerto de Santa María and Sanlúcar de Barrameda. The last is the traditional home of a type of pale, delicate dry sherry called manzanilla.

The production process for sherry is one of the most complicated of any fortified wine. When the new white wine is made, it

TIO PEPE
Muy Seco is the very driest style of sherry

OTHER NAMES
Spain: Jerez *France*: Xérès

is fermented until fully dry, and then transferred into large butts. Some sherries, the ones that are destined to end up as the pale dry style known as fino (or manzanilla), develop a film of yeast culture called *flor* on the surface of the wine. In some barrels, the layer of *flor* dies out because it has consumed all the remaining nutrients in the wine, whereupon it breaks up and sinks to the bottom of the butt.

HARVEYS BRISTOL CREAM
A big-selling brown cream sherry

HOW TO SERVE
Fino and manzanilla, and the sweetened pale sherries, should be served very well chilled, preferably from a freshly opened bottle. In Spain, they think nothing of drinking a bottle of dry sherry as we would a table wine. The other styles should be served at room temperature. Finos are brilliant aperitifs, old olorosos best at the other end of the meal.

With the subsequent greater exposure to the air, the colour of the wine deepens through oxidation, and the style known as amontillado results.

Some wines develop no *flor* at all and go on to turn a deep, woody brown colour. These are oloroso sherries. The fortification of the wine varies according to the style. Fino may be fortified to only 15% ABV, whereas oloroso is generally bottled at around 20%. At this stage, all of the wines are naturally dry, and some – the true connoisseur's sherries – will be bottled in that condition after ageing in cask.

Many commercial sherries, however, are made sweet by the addition of a quantity of *mistela*, the juice of raisined grapes to which grape spirit has been added. The best sweet sherries are sweetened with PX, which stands for Pedro Ximénez, the name of a grape variety whose berries are left to dry in the sun until loss of moisture has concentrated their sugars to an almost unbelievable degree. Some houses bottle some of their PX separately as a speciality product.

Other countries that produce sherry-style wines are Australia (which makes about the best outside Jerez), the United States, South Africa and Cyprus. Within Spain itself, there are two other regions near Jerez that produce similar fortified wines in the same range of styles, but they are not as distinguished as sherry. One is Montilla-Morilés, the other the virtually forgotten Condado de Huelva.

Spain's other great, now sadly nearly extinct, fortified wine is Málaga, made around the Mediterranean port of that name. Its finest wines are deep brown, caramel-sweet creations of great power, once hugely popular in Britain, now forsaken by fashion.

TASTES GOOD WITH

Dry sherries are good with salted nuts such as almonds, with piquant nibbles such as olives and salty fish like anchovies, and with Serrano ham or its Mediterranean equivalents. The sweet old olorosos are wonderful with rich, dark fruitcake and hard Spanish sheep's milk cheeses such as Manchego.

EMVA CREAM
A Cypriot wine, no longer labelled as "sherry"

VERMOUTH

VERMOUTH IS AS FAR removed from the natural produce of the vine as it is possible for a fortified wine to get. Not only is it strengthened with spirit, but it is also heavily aromatized with herbs and botanical ingredients in order to make a distinctive type of drink that is usually intended for drinking – either mixed or unmixed – as an aperitif. There is no particular connoisseurship of vermouth, as there is for aged sherries and vintage ports. This is an everyday product made to a consistent and unchanging recipe by each manufacturer.

The presence in vermouth of that cocktail of herbs

HOW TO SERVE
A drop or two only of dry French vermouth is needed for the perfect dry Martini or Vodkatini.

All these drinks should be served as aperitifs or at the cocktail hour. Vermouth is not as fragile once opened as pale dry sherry tends to be. It doesn't have to be drunk up within a few days, and is able to withstand extremes of temperature far more hardily than the other light fortified wines.

*MARTINI
EXTRA DRY
The top brand of
vermouth inter-
nationally*

and roots alerts us to the fact that this was originally a medicinal drink. That said, the practice of adding herbs to wine goes back to ancient Greek times, when the extra ingredients may have been put in as much to disguise the taste of spoiled wine as for their curative powers. A popular early additive was wormwood, villain of the piece when absinthe was outlawed, yet much prized as a tonic for the stomach from classical antiquity through to medieval times and the beginnings of distillation in Europe.

As far as a drink identifiable as the precursor of modern vermouth is concerned, we have to travel back to the 1500s in order to find a merchant called d'Alessio selling a wormwood wine in Piedmont (now in northwest Italy). The inspiration had come from similar German products, probably produced on a domestic scale, and it is from the German word for wormwood, *Wermuth*, that the modern English word is derived. It was already popular in England by the middle years of the following century.

Two centres of vermouth production came to be established. One was in d'Alessio's part of Italy, close to the alpine hills that were a handy wild source of the various botanical ingredients that went into the wine, and the other over the border in eastern and southeastern France. As the big commercial companies were founded, two distinct styles of vermouth emerged, one pale and dry with pronounced bitterness, the other red and sweet and not quite so bitter. The former was the style associated with France, the latter with Italy. So ingrained did these

NOILLY PRAT
A bone-dry
vermouth
produced in
the south of
France

FLAVOURINGS

May include quinine, coriander seeds, cloves, juniper, ginger, dried orange and lemon peel, hyssop, camomile, raspberries, rose-petals, and so on.

definitions become that, even now, drinkers still refer to "French" and "Italian" to mean dry and sweet respectively, when these may not necessarily be the geographical origins.

In fact, sweet and dry vermouths are made in both countries, and indeed elsewhere, including the United States. Brands vary according to the number and type of the herbal ingredients added, but the basic style remains the same from one batch to the next. Cloves, cinnamon, quinine, citrus peels, ginger, perhaps a touch of wormwood still (although the banning of absinthe sharply decreased the amount of wormwood that was considered acceptable in other drinks) are typical elements in the pot-pourri of aromatizers that go into the modern vermouths.

As with many of the traditional liqueurs, the medicinal image of vermouth was – by the onset of the 20th century – something of an albatross around its neck, rather than a marketing opportunity. It was once again the cocktail era that rode to its rescue, finding multifarious uses for both styles of vermouth. After all, if the traditional dry Martini was destined to be the only use to which dry vermouth could be put behind the bar – one drop at a time – then not a great deal of it was ever going to be sold. Because it is quite as perfumed, in its way, as gin, vermouth proved hugely versatile in mixed drinks, and the demand for it

today – thanks in part to the big proprietary brands – remains reasonably steady.

The bulk-producing Italian firm of Martini e Rossi, based at Turin, is still the vermouth name that springs most readily to mind for consumers today. Other Italian producers are Riccadonna, Cinzano and Gancia. In France, the Marseillan producer Noilly Prat makes one of the more highly regarded dry vermouths, but also has a sweeter style. The region of Chambéry in eastern France has been awarded the *appellation contrôlée* for its vermouths, which include a strawberry-flavoured fruit version called Chambéryzette. As well as red and white styles

CINZANO BIANCO
Hugely popular brand of sweet white vermouth

CARPANO PUNT E MES
A deep red vermouth produced at Turin

MIXING
Bronx: Shake a measure of gin, half a measure each of dry and sweet red vermouth and the juice of no more than a quarter of an orange with ice, and strain into a cocktail glass.

of vermouth, there is a golden or amber variant, and a rosé.

Other similar branded products include Lillet of Bordeaux, owned by one of the classed-growth claret châteaux, which blends a proportion of fruit juice in with the wine base along with the customary herbs; the French Dubonnet, a red or white sweet vermouth also full of highly appetizing quinine bitterness; and Punt e Mes, a similar but dark-coloured Italian product that combines sweetening and bittering elements in intriguing balance.

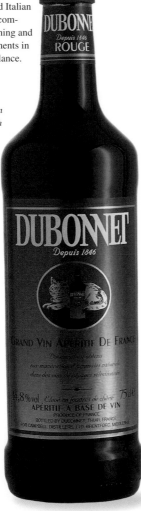

DUBONNET
The red version mixes well with lemonade

HOW IT IS MADE

A low-alcohol, mostly white wine is produced and may be allowed a short period of ageing. For the sweeter styles of vermouth, it then has a quantity of sugar syrup added to it before the fortification with spirit. This is usually grape spirit but may occasionally also be derived from vegetable sources such as sugar beet. The wine is then transferred into large barrels or tanks to which the dried aromatising ingredients have already been added. From time to time, the mixture is stirred up manually with wooden paddles. After absorption of the flavourings, the vermouth will be bottled at around 17% ABV. Some producers insist their vermouths will continue to age in the bottle for a couple of years if kept. There are no vintage vermouths.

TASTES GOOD WITH

Dry vermouths are particularly useful in the kitchen for adding to sauces to accompany fish. The herbal ingredients in the vermouth add an attractive savoury note to the dish. A seasoned reduction of Noilly Prat, lemon juice and single cream is a fine way to treat good white fish such as sole or turbot.

MIXING

Bentley: Shake generous equal measures of calvados and red Dubonnet with plenty of ice, and strain into a cocktail glass. **Midsummer Night**: Shake equal measures of gin and Punt e Mes with a half-measure of cassis and ice. Strain into a cocktail glass.

NON-ALCOHOLIC MIXERS

ALTHOUGH MANY of the drinks talked about in this book are commonly drunk unmixed, such as single malt whiskies, aged brandies and rums, and the fortified wines, the great majority of them would not be consumed at all were it not for non-alcoholic mixers. Some of these are so familiar as to need no explanation; others may be more rarely used, but nonetheless constitute an important element in the mixed drink and cocktail repertoire.

FRUIT JUICES

Of all the fruit juices, orange is probably the most important for mixing with single spirit shots, most notably with the white spirits that don't muddy its colour. To the cocktail-maker, freshly squeezed lemon juice is undoubtedly the most versatile ingredient. The juice of lemons has the uncanny ability to accentuate the flavours of other fruits, almost in the manner of a seasoning (try tasting a fresh fruit purée with and without lemon juice to demonstrate this point), and so it complements the fruit-flavoured liqueurs very well. Additionally, its sourness mitigates the syrupy sweetness of many of the classic liqueurs. Lime juice is yet more sour and is used in drinks that should have a particularly biting tang. Pineapple makes a sweetly exotic element in some rum-based mixtures.

ORANGE JUICE

FRESHLY SQUEEZED LEMON JUICE

SPARKLING BEVERAGES

To achieve the diluting effects of water without changing flavour, and add a refreshing sparkle to a mixture, soda water is the required ingredi-ent. At one time, no bar (or home for that matter) was complete without a soda-siphon. They were charged with tablets of sodium bicarbonate and dispensed a stream of bubbling water through a pressurized nozzle. Nowadays, there is effectively no difference between bottled or canned soda and carbonated mineral water.

TONIC WATER

Tonic water and gin go together like Fred Astaire and Ginger Rogers. A sweetened fizzy water flavoured with the bittering component, quinine, tonic is medicinally named for the anti-malarial properties it demonstrated in tropical climes. It is useful not just with gin, but with vodka and even calvados –

SODA-SIPHON

WATER

The simplest of all mixers is the one that dilutes the strength of ardent spirits without altering the character of their basic flavour. Water is indispensable to whisky drinkers, who claim that it enhances rather than mutes the aromatic per-sonalities of their favoured spirit. Water softens the olfactory impact of the alcohol while allowing the complexities of grain, peat and wood to announce themselves.

Pastis drinkers use plain water, too, for the cloudiness that gives the drinks their collec-tive name can only be obtained by mixing. In all cases, good spring water or mineral water is preferable to heavily chlorinated tap – especially so in the case of Highland and Lowland malts.

wherever the dryness of a drink can be made the more appetizing with bitterness.

Lemonade should not be thought of solely as a children's drink, as it provides a useful way of administering citric sour-ness and fizz to a long drink. The best lemonades for bar use are not as sweet as the kids may like them, and some are actually still, in which case you may just as well use lemon juice and a pinch of sugar.

LEMONADE

All cola is derived from the invention of Coca-Cola in the United States in the late 19th century by one John Pemberton. It was originally intended as a stimulating tonic drink, and included the ground nuts of the cola tree, along with crushed coca leaves. The latter are also the source of the drug cocaine, which came to be frowned on in the early years of this century, and so Coca-Cola removed them from the recipe. Rum and neutral vodka seem to be the main spirits with which cola mixes most happily, coffee-flavoured Kahlúa and Tia Maria its closest liqueur companions.

COCA-COLA

Ginger ale or ginger beer also has its uses, with Scotch for example, but perhaps most famously with vodka as a Moscow Mule. Vodka-maker Smirnoff now makes a pre-mixed version of this drink.

SYRUPS

Cocktail-making would not be quite what it is without the availability of a range of flavoured non-alcoholic syrups to add complexity and interest to a drink. Of these, the most famous is grenadine, used to give a strong red colouring to otherwise clear mixtures, and to create the red-orange-yellow colour spectrum in the classic Tequila Sunrise. Grenadine is made principally from the juice of the pomegranate, the peculiar Asiatic fruit that looks like a thick-skinned onion but, when cut, reveals a mass of jewel-like seeds within. It is thick, ruby-coloured and intensely sweet; some brands are made with a small alcohol quotient, but no more than about 3% ABV.

Orgeat is another little-seen syrup that was once used very widely in cocktails. Its flavour-ing element was almonds and it added that telltale taste of marzipan to a drink, even when used in very sparing quantities. Its name derives from the French word *orge*, meaning barley, which was once one of its ingredients.

Other syrups, flavoured with a whole green-grocer's shop of exotic ingredients, are now available. Pineapple, apricot, strawberry, banana, even kiwi-fruit are produced, and can add an appetizing dash of fruit flavour to a mixed drink, without the extra alcohol that liqueurs bring.

In addition to the flavoured syrups, it is also possible to buy a bottled neutral sugar syrup called gomme, but as it consists only of sugar and water, you may as well make your own.

GRENADINE
The principal flavour of this red syrup is pomegranate

aGOMME
This is simply a straight sugar and water syrup

ORGEAT
An almond-flavoured syrup once widely used

GINGER BEER

A traditional English summer concoction, ginger beer works well as a mixer for basic Scotch, and with vodka for a Moscow Mule.

INDEX

PHOTOGRAPHS

All photographs by
David Jordan and
Janine Hosegood
except those supplied
by Cephas Picture
Library: pp. 6 and 7
Aviemore Photogra-
phy; pp. 8 and 9 Mick
Rock; p. 12 (top left)
Nigel Blythe, (bottom
left) Mick Rock and
(right) Stuart Boreham;
p. 13 Stuart Boreham;
p. 60 (top) John
Heinrich, (bottom left)
Tripelon/Jarry and
(bottom right) Herve
Champollion;
pp. 61, 108 and 109
Mick Rock.

NOTES

NOTES

NOTES

NOTES